English You Need

H. M. Dobinson

Nelson

Contents

1
The English we speak

16 year olds can't speak good English, says employer

Schools slammed for bad teaching

Mr T. Jones, Personnel Manager of Seaton's largest engineering works, said today that the 16 year olds he interviews can't speak good English. 'The way they talk when they come to us for interview is disgusting,' he told a group of teachers at the Town Hall. 'It's time you lot taught them something.'

Headmistress angry

Miss S. Shaw, Headmistress of Seaton Comprehensive School, was stung to reply, 'Has Mr Jones not got round to asking these young men and ladies to explain how much they know about . . .'

Clash of canny sides

**Head your work
1.1   What I have learnt at school**

1   What do you think you have learnt at school? Which of these possible answers would be true?
- I have learnt how to do sums.
- I have learnt how to tell the time.
- I have learnt about how our country is run.
- I have learnt about die-stamping and operating a power press.
- I have learnt how to handle a telephone switchboard.
What other answers could there be?

2   What do you think are the signs of being well educated? Which of these answers would be true?
- Being able to work things out.
- Being able to ring up a bill on a cash register.
- Being able to use a lot of long words.
- Being able to talk clearly.
What other answers could there be?

3

Head your work
1.2 Ways of talking

1 Who do you take after when you talk?
Your grandparents?
Your mother?
Your father?
Your friends at school?
Your teachers?
A mixture of them all?
A pop star?
The television people?

2 Do adults you know often change the way they speak?
At what times and places do they speak differently?

3 Who do you think the pupil in this piece would take after in talking?

4

4   Did the old sort of education with a cane really help Dad learn good English?

5   Do you think Dad would have been so quick to talk of violence if he had been better at arguing with words?

1.3   Word match

A dictionary tells you many things. One of these is how to say a word if the spelling might put you off. It can save you making some silly mistakes. Sea-cadets and sailors might laugh if you called a bosun a boat swain. But that's how it's spelt.

Letting the dictionary help you
All longer words can be broken into different bits. Each bit is said in one go. Each bit is called a syllable. A word like 'biscuit' has two syllables — 'bis' and 'kit'.

a) Syllable count
How many syllables are there in these words? Write down the words in the bits that make each syllable. One is done for you.

people	syllable	
television	dictionary	dic-tion-a-ry
grandparents	differently	
government	anyway	
teaches	comprehensive	
recipe	cupboard	

In almost all our words one bit is said with more of a puff than the rest of the word. This is called the stressed syllable. A dictionary marks the end of a stressed syllable with a little sign like this '.

b) Stressed syllables in common words
Be a dictionary writer yourself and put a mark after the stressed syllable in each of these words. One is done for you:

longer	em-ploy'-er
sailors	personnel
cadets	disgusting
mistakes	examine
spelling	register

c) Stressed syllables in less common words
Now use a dictionary to look up where the stress comes in the words in the next list. Find out what they mean at the same time, if you don't know them all:

hypocaust
hypocrisy
hypodermic
hypochondria

**Head your work
1.3   Word match.
How to say words I
don't know**

In English spelling we have letters or groups of letters that stand for most sounds we need ('a' as in 'hat'; 'b' as in 'Bob'; 'sh' as in 'ship'). But strangely enough we have no special letter that stands for a very common little sound — the sound you can hear at the ends of words like:

Peter, Rita, doctor

or in the little word 'a' when it's not important ('Would you like *a* cup of tea?'), or in many other unimportant bits of words. Some dictionaries try to show you how to say a word by printing this sound with an e upside down like this: ə.

d) The little sound ə
If you use this how would you write these words?

farmer
machine
flavour
Saturday
author

The broad top edge of this boat is the gunwale. What are the other parts called?

e) Saying some trick words

Trick words	Rhyming words
gunwale	tinny
moustache	funnel
hic-cough	Lassie
chassis	pick-up
blackguard	laggard
guinea	marsh

Write down the list of trick words. Start a new line for each word. Now use a dictionary and find out how you should say each word. Write down what the dictionary tells you against each word that you look up and then choose a word from the other list which sounds much the same (rhymes) and write that down on the same line.

6

1.4 How many languages can you talk?

Here are six ways of greeting someone. Which would you use for each of the situations shown here?

EH UP! BEN.

HELLO GRAN.

GOOD DAY, YOUR MAJESTY.

WATCHER, MATE!

COME IN DARLING!

MORNING SIR.

What other situations like these can you think of? (How about at work?) What would you say in each?

1.5 What do you expect?

Do you expect the other drivers to keep to the left of the road?
Do you expect television programmes to begin on time?
Do you expect water from the tap when you turn it on?
Do you expect people to talk sense?
Do you expect people to talk good English?
Here are three little points that most people expect to hear at a time like an interview:

1 Words said clearly, and the whole word used, not just a bit of it. Don't shorten it.
2 Answers in whole sentences, not just mumbles and grunts.
3 Questions asked with well-chosen words.

Here are some of the things that one of the pupils said when he went for an interview with Mr Jones in Seaton. What were the things that Mr Jones was complaining about?

Head your work
1.5 What John should have said

Can you write down what John should have said? You may be able to save Mr Jones some of his questions by giving John longer answers.

Mr Jones	Am I right in thinking you would like to apply for an apprenticeship with us?
John	Ya.
Mr Jones	How old are you now, John?
John	Sixteen.
Mr Jones	Are you doing examinations in school this summer?
John	Yep.

HU. DUNNO.

Mr Jones	Which ones are they?
John	C.S.E. English and Maths, Art, Geog. and Teck D.
Mr Jones	What is Teck D, John?
John	Um. Teck Drawing. You use a lot of rulers and things and you draw things all over the paper.
Mr Jones	What made you apply for an apprenticeship with us?
John	Me mate works 'ere.
Mr Jones	Oh, I see. Is he an apprentice, too?
John	Hu. Dunno.
Mr Jones	What is his name?

Head your work
1.6 Write away!
(and the title)

1.6 Write away!

Choose one of the following topics and write a piece of about 200 words about it.

1 **The things grandparents say.** Do they have a fuddy-duddy way of talking? Do some of their pet words make you laugh?

2 **The way my teacher talks.** Are there things your teacher says that seem strange to you? Things you can't understand? Things you wouldn't say yourself?

3 **Those people on the box.** Choose any two people you often see on television and put down what you notice about the way they talk.

1.7 Controversy

Head your work
1.7 Does it matter how we talk?

1 Should people mind how we talk?
2 Whose job is it to teach you how to talk?
3 Was Mr Jones right to blame the schools?
4 Do you care how someone talks to you?
5 Do you care how they talk on television?

1.8 Read all about it

Head your work
1.8 Fun with Silky

Have you read how Silky tricked young Michael? It's in Michael Baldwin's book *Grandad with Snails*. Have you known people of your grandparents age who were full of fun like Silky? What tricks do they like to play? Perhaps you have a younger brother like Michael, or a friend of yours may have one. Can you make up another story about Silky and Michael? Perhaps Michael would like to know how Silky got white hair — what trick might Silky play?

Riddle
What can you eat as often as you like, but will never fill you up?

'Words' — when you admit a mistake, you eat your words.

1.9 Crossword number one

Copy this crossword frame with a centimetre square and see how quickly you can complete it. The answers to clues with a * are words that have been used in this chapter.

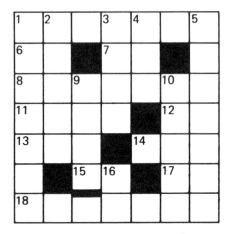

Clues across

* 1 A word we often say when we greet someone in the morning (7).
* 6 A short little word that means a thing, and comes at the end of 'limit' (2).
* 7 Not off (2).
* 8 In an interview remember to say the whole word; just to say Teck D is to ——— it too much (7).
 11 Eleven players playing together (4).
 12 Second half of the word 'claw' (2).
*13 The lesson where you learn painting and drawing (3).
 14 First half of the word 'italic' (3).
*15 A grunt of disgust or puzzlement (2).
 17 Middle two letters of the word 'sell' (2).
 18 To look at something closely – perhaps to find out how much you know (7).

Clues down

* 1 Something done wrong, such as a word said wrong (7).
* 2 Not this one but the ——— one (5).
 3 The first half of the word 'normally' (4).
 4 Second half of the word 'splint' (3).
* 5 The top edge of a boat's side; it rhymes with funnel (7).
 9 A sort of swearing used in court (4).
*10 What you've done with your words when you've taken them back (5).
*16 A short sound we make when we can't think of the next word (2).

2
Filing and alphabetical order

2.1   Alphabetical order

Everywhere you go things are put in alphabetical order. How good are you at using it? Can you put things in order yourself?

Which of these things would you expect to find in alphabetical order? Why would the other things probably be in some other order?

1   Names in a telephone book.
2   Words in an index.
3   Stopping places on a bus timetable.
4   Street names in a street plan index.
5   Names in a class list.
6   Recipes in a book.
7   Teams in a league table.
8   Record cards at the doctor's.
9   Insurance policies with policy numbers.
10   Books in a library.

Do you know the alphabet by heart? Which way would you turn in a telephone book if you opened a page at *s* when you wanted a name beginning with *v*? How far would you expect to go?

Many people are not really sure of bits in the alphabet like that, but it is useful to be able to remember just a bit without saying the lot. Try learning it in bits like this:

When you are looking for something in alphabetical order, you may find many words beginning with *s*. They are arranged in the order of the second letters. You may find many words beginning with *sh*. They are arranged on the third letters. And so on to the end of each word. Can you put these lists into alphabetical order?

11   swim sale soup send show
12   shake shrug shut shelf shine
13   shrank shrunk shrink shred shrew
14   squads satisfaction stumbled insect radiance
15   delta spiral recipe mechanics lever

11

There was a young lady called Stephanie,
Who insisted on putting g before f and e,
She put h after p,
And n before e,
But at least she could spell Persephone.

2.2 The clerk who tried too hard

Head your work
2.2 The Clerk who tried too hard

1   Here are some other files that were usually kept near the Tax Demand file in Shirley's drawer. What order do you think she expected them to be in: Trade Accounts, Tax Demand, Stationery Orders, Regulations, V.A.T.?

2   Ken might have thought of some other headings as well as 'money' to put the file under. Which of these would have been possible headings? What is wrong with the three headings that won't do?
Accounts, Inland Revenue, Profits, Bank, Post Office, Inspector of Taxes.

2.3 Word match

The words in a dictionary are in alphabetical order. But even so you could miss some of them.

This is because some dictionaries put words that have the same stem (group of letters) in the same block of print. To save space the letters that have already been printed in heavy type are not put down again. The dictionary just puts a ~ to mean 'repeat the letters in heavy print'. So the word you want may just look like this: ~ ly. Remember to look through all the block of print after you have found the first set of letters in a word.

The only words that will be split in this way are words that have bits on the end. 'Sidewalk' has '-walk' on the end of 'side', 'cheaply' has 'ly' on the end of 'cheap'.

What are the endings on these words? What are the 'base words'?

1   singer
2   fisherman
3   hairdresser
4   lover
5   sportsman

Now look these words up in a dictionary. What 'base-words' can you find them under?

6   illumination
7   regressive
8   radiance
9   intermittent
10 particularly

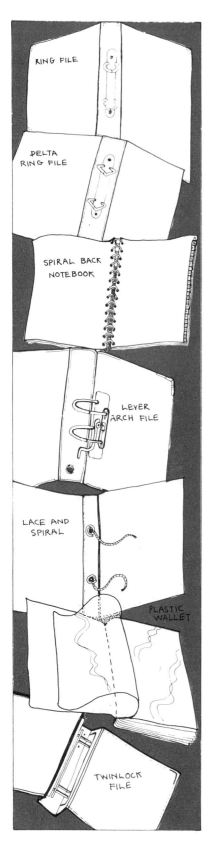

2.4 Ways of filing

When you go to work, there will be many things to keep in files. For example, if you work in an engineering firm there will be records of machine parts, suppliers of metal, letters received and copies of replies, etc.

While you are at school there are lots of things to put in files – your work from this book; coursework in other subjects; things at home for your own interest.

There are many different sorts of files and ways of filing. Study this list and then answer the questions below.

Ring file
Stiff covers. Not very fat.
Pull the ring and it springs open. Snap it shut.
Put in pages anywhere you like.
Pages at top and bottom bend and tear near the rings.

Delta ring file
Like a ring file but a special shaped ring to cut down the bending of end pages.

Spiral back notebook
Pages fixed in a spiral.
Will open flat wherever you like.
Cannot put pages in or lift them out.
'Thumb cuts' in the right hand edge help you find each letter of the alphabet quickly if arranged in alphabetical order.

Lever arch file
About 8 or 9 cms thick.
A lever opens the metal rods that hold the pages.
You can put in pages where you like.
Edges do not get damaged.

Lace and spiral
Can be very thin.
Thread the lace through your papers.
Tie the lace on the spiral.
Papers do not get damaged.
You have to take all the papers out if you want to put one at the bottom.

Plastic wallet
Expensive folder.
Clear plastic wallet with pockets.
You put your papers in the pocket and read them through the plastic.
Does not hold many papers.
Papers don't get worn or dirty even if your fingers are dirty when you're in the middle of a job.

Twinlock file
A special locking sort of lever arch file.
Keeps papers very safe.
Expensive very strong folder.

Which of these folders would you choose for these jobs, and why would you choose it?

1   You have a few sheets of paper that mechanics would need again and again.

2   You are going to have a large number of papers, and you want to be able to add new papers in different parts.

3   You have a small number of papers that you keep on adding to, but it doesn't matter what order they are in so long as they don't take too much room on your desk.

4   You want to write down the addresses of all your friends and be able to find them again quickly.

5   The boss asks you to get a strong folder for some very important papers and says the firm will pay you back when you bring the receipt.

2.5   Filing your work from this book

You may like to use file paper for your work from this book.

Make the first page a **title page**.
Make the next page a **table of contents**. You will have to decide how you are going to arrange your work.
You might like to keep it in **chapter order**. If so, your table of contents will be in the same order as the chapters in this book.
You might like to file it by what sort of work it is. You will find that in every chapter:

section 3 is called   **Word match**
section 6 is called   **Write away**
section 7 is called   **Controversy**
section 8 is called   **Read all about it**
section 9 is a   **Crossword.**

The work in sections 1, 2, 4, and 5 is **various**. So you might like to use these divisions for your work.

Next you will need **divider cards** for the chapters or sections you choose. Coloured paper can often do as well as a stiff card for this.

Each piece of work you do should be done in your best handwriting. Put a clear heading on the work. Be careful to put down the section number given in the margin.

Before you begin on each sheet, plan your layout carefully. How much of the sheet do you expect to fill? Try to put your work down in a way that makes the page look nice when you have finished.

2.6 Write away!

**Head your work
2.6 Write away!
(and the title)**

Choose one of the following topics and write a piece about 200 words long about it.

1 **Tidy up your bedroom!** Do you know anyone who gets the bedroom into a mess, with clothes, records, sportsgear and magazines all over the place? What does it look like? How would you suggest the things should be put away?

2 **Mr Messy and Mr Tidy.** Some people make so much mess that they could be called 'Mr Messy' and some people spend so much time tidying that they could be called 'Mr Tidy'. Do you know anyone like that? Which one do you like best? Does the other one irritate you?

3 **Towns old and new.** Old parts of the town were not usually planned at all. They are often very untidy, with all sorts of buildings side by side. Some new towns have been planned so much that they have rows and rows of buildings all the same. Describe one or two places you know. What sort of town do you like best?

2.7 Controversy

**Head your work
2.7 Controversy:
organising and filing**

1 Telephone books have too many names in them. They shouldn't try to cover such a big area.

2 You cannot get on unless you are organised.

3 Some people waste so much time on organising things that they never get anything done.

4 Schools should give the older pupils some money and let them buy their own files and folders, so they could get the sort they like.

5 The Armed Forces are well organised, but we don't want to live like soldiers, bossed around all the time.

2.8 Read all about it

More and more things are being done by computers. If you arrange words in order well enough, a computer can even be made to talk.

Are **people** being arranged in order too much? Read the story of *The Pedestrian* by Ray Bradbury. How many of your class walk just for the fun of walking? Do any groups you know go hiking or orienteering? As more and more people get mopeds and cars, could it be that walking for fun will be even less common? Do you think it odd if someone you know has not got television at home? Is there something strange about people who cannot be 'filed' in our 'index' easily, because of things they like that are different?

Can you make up a story about habits that are changing and how even an interest of your own could come to seem strange — strange perhaps to make your own music, to make your own bread, or stranger still not to have a pocket calculator?

Riddle
Why couldn't the robber steal the papers from the safe?
Because he couldn't find the right file.

*COMES TO VISIT THE EARTH,
HE GOES INTO THE LIBRARY...*

WHAT HAVE YOU EARTHMEN WRITTEN IN YOUR BOOKS ABOUT MARS?

SPACE TRAVEL IS DEWEY NUMBER 629·1388, SIR.

WHY DON'T YOU PUT MARS IN ALPHABETICAL ORDER?

2.9 Crossword number two

Clues across

* 1   A piece of wire wound round and round. (6)
* 7   Odd and unexplained (when a file goes missing) (5).
* 8   Another word for 'I' when I'm not in charge (2).
  9   Very unkind (5).
*11   All the letters we use, put down in order (8).
*14   Ask for something in a way you are not allowed to refuse (6).
*16   Short word for 'thank you' (2).
 17   Grass round the edges of a pavement or road (6).

*19   The outside bits of a sheet of paper (5).
*21   Sharon's helpful suggestion was to ask, 'Have you __ __? (5, 3)

Clues down

* 1   A group of people together, perhaps in the army (5).
 2   First two letters of the word 'push' (2).
 3   These two letters stand for 'id est', which mean 'that is' (2)
 4   If a car battery has gone flat you need to _____ it at a garage (8).
* 5   Put in order (8).

* 6   A special shape for a ring file – like a big Greek D (5).
* 8   Goes to see someone (5).
 10   Last two letters of the word 'scrub' (2).
*12   A bar used to move something else (5).
*13   These two letters mean 'post meridiem' or 'past midday' (2).
*15   You sit at it for writing; it may have drawers (4).
 18   First half of the word 'editor' (3).
*20   The other way from 'off' (2).

3
Wise spelling methods

3.1 The initial teaching alphabet

> ſhis iſ printed in ſhe iniſhial teeçhiŋ alfabet, ſhe purpoſ ov whiçh iſ not, aſ miet beε suppœſd, tω reform our spelliŋ, but tω improωv ſhe lerniŋ ov reεdiŋ. it iſ intended ſhat when ſhe beginner iſ flωent in ſhis meεdium heε ſhωd beε confiend tω reεdiŋ in ſhe tradiſhonal alfabet.

Have you ever seen writing like this?
It's English all right.
What's happened to it?
Think of these pairs of words:

tω	to
improωv	improve
ſhωd	should
flωent	fluent

This sort of writing is called the initial teaching alphabet.
It has been used for teaching reading in many infant schools.
1   Do you know anyone who has learnt on this system?
2   Are there any books printed like this in the local bookshop?
3   Can you see why some teachers like five-year olds to begin their reading lessons with i.t.a.? Why should it be easier?
4   Some children get muddled because everything else they see written is not printed in i.t.a. Some of them still find spelling difficult when they are 15 years old.
5   Do you think i.t.a. is a good idea or not?

3.2 We say it differently but we spell it the same

Sometimes someone does try to write English in the way a particular person speaks it. It is not always easy to read. Try reading this verse from a poem:

Wi' lightsome heart I pu'd a rose
  Frae aff its thorny tree,
And my fause luver staw my rose
  But left the thorn wi' me.

We can read things easily and quickly when they are spelt in the way we are used to. The right full stops, capital letters and commas (which is called *punctuation*) also helps us to make sense of the writing quickly.

'What's inside it?' asked the Mole, wriggling with curiosity.
'There's cold chicken inside it,' replied the Rat briefly; 'coldtonguecoldhamcoldbeefpickledgherkinssaladfrench rollscresssandwidgespottedmeatgingerbeerlemonade sodawater — '

Head your work
3.2 Writing things the usual way

Try to write out the above two passages with the spelling and punctuation we usually expect (words to help you with the verse are: *with*, *pulled*, *from*, *off*, *false*, *lover*, *stole*). They should then be much easier to read!

3.3 Word match

Dictionaries can help us with the spelling as well as the meaning of words.

Most of all our words begin with the letter you would expect from the sound of the word. You can usually have a good idea of the second or third letter from the sound also. The problem in spelling is often in the middle or at the end of the word.

If you know the first two or three letters you can look in the right part of the dictionary. The way to find the spelling you want is to try two or three possibilities.
Firstly, if you are wondering how to spell 'friend' you can hear it must begin with **fr**. You might expect it to be spelt **frend** but you can soon see that that word is not in the dictionary. You might remember there is an i somewhere so you might try **freind**. As that fails also, you would try **friend** and find it. Third time lucky!

Head your work
3.3   Word match:
corrected spellings

Here are some words that have spelling mistakes of this kind. If you cannot correct them straightaway, try using a dictionary to check the spellings:

1	dictionery	6	machinary
2	popullation	7	automobil
3	assosiation	8	apoint
4	recippy	9	inteligence
5	romanse	10	athleticks

Secondly, a dictionary will help you with spelling a word when one has put a bit on the end — do you have to double the last letter or anything special like that? This information is usually given in brackets just after the word, such as **wet (-tt-)** means that the longer words are

wetting and **wetted**.

Use a dictionary (if you need to) to check what happens to the spellings of these words when -ing is added to them:
11   regret
12   forget
13   disappoint
14   write
15   control

Thirdly, there is sometimes a problem when a word begins with a letter you cannot hear. There are few of these words in English, and you will probably know most of them already as 'trick words'. The letters most often found silent are **g**, **k**, and **p**. So if you have a trick word like gnat (a small fly) and you can't find it under **nat**, you can look under **pnat**, **knat**, and **gnat** and you will have found it — you don't have to try the whole alphabet.

Here are some more trick words. The only spelling mistake in them is the missing first letter. How are they really spelt?

16   neel (on your knees)
17   nome (model in the garden)
18   nife (to cut with)
19   naw (with your teeth)
20   tarmigan (a big bird from mountain country)
21   sychiatrist (treats worried people)
22   nowledge (learnt in your head)
23   sychologist (measures how clever you are)
24   nuckle (on your fingers)
25   nash (your teeth together)

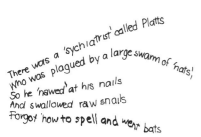

There was a 'sychiatrist' called Platts
Who was plagued by a large swarm of 'nats'
So he 'nawed' at his nails
And swallowed raw snails
Forgot how to spell and went bats

3.4 Why punctuation matters

- Spaces between words,
- Capital letters for names and new sentences,
- Full stops at the end of sentences,
- Commas where one should make a pause for breath,
  or for separating things in a list,
- Speech marks round the words someone actually said,
- Question marks at the end of a question,
- Apostrophes for missing letters,
  and for belonging words like Anne's,
  but not for: his, hers, its, ours, yours, theirs.

The punctuation rules listed here all matter, and help us to understand what is written.

**Head your work
3.4 Putting in the punctuation**

Write out this piece with the correct punctuation marks in. You will need to use 22 marks altogether, all of which can be found in the list above.

peter and jane were going to go to the disco to their surprise altiner and vilma were going to go too two pairs is too many to go in my sports car said peter you will have to take your bike too ive told you the way to go to get there altiner agreed to take his bike too

3.5   Some key spelling rules

Here are some of the most important spelling rules.
Do you know them all?

1   **Dropping the last 'e'.** If a word ends with an **e** and
you are going to add **ed** or **ing** or another group of letters
on the end, you will usually **drop the 'e'** before you add
the others:

complete   completing   completed   completion

2   **Doubling the last consonant.** Many words that end
with *just one* consonant* double this before putting extra
letters on the end:

rivet   rivetting   rivetted

3   **i before e except straight after c.** In words where
the two letters **ie** go together to stand for the same sound
as **ee** in **feet**, the order of these letters follows the rule in
this rhyme:

field   ceiling   chief

4   **y changes to i before a vowel.** In words that end
with a consonant and then a **y**, the **y** changes to **i** if you
are going to add a vowel (except **i**) on the end:

fly   flies   flying

**Head your work
3.5   Right spellings that
fit the rules**

All these words have spelling mistakes in them. Write them
out without mistakes, and say what rule helps you to know
how to spell them.

1	replyes	6	forgeting
2	reciept	7	cheiftain
3	regreted	8	forgeryes
4	competeing	9	receiveing
5	writeing	10	unbelieveing

3.6   Write away

**Head your work
3.6   Write away!
(and the title)**

Choose one of the following topics and write a piece about
200 words long about it.

1   **My worst words.** The words you can't spell, and the
troubles they give you. Things you have been told off for,
and how you've been told off. The troubles you've had
with spelling.

2   **School.** What's wrong with school, and the things you
have to learn, the books you use, and so on? And what
would you do to put them right?

3   **Flat out till leaving age.** All the things you would
like to manage before you leave school, and the things
you'd like to be able to get better at.

* There are two types of letters –
vowels and consonants. **Vo**wels stand
for the sounds we make with our
voice, and these are **A E I O U** and
sometimes **Y**. Consonants are all the
other letters in the alphabet and they
stand for the sounds made with lips,
tongue or throat.

3.7 Controversy

1   Teachers shouldn't be allowed to do experiments like the initial teaching alphabet experiment with their pupils.
2   Who is 'right' about how something is spelt?
3   How much does it matter about spelling? Are we right to care when we see lots of mistakes in writing? Is it a sign of how well you have been educated?
4   The initial teaching alphabet is better than ordinary spelling and everyone should use it.
5   They never taught us enough in the Junior Schools. That's why some students find things hard now.

3.8   Read all about it

One poet who has bent the rules of punctuation and spacing to serve his own ends is e.e. cummings. Have you read any of his poems? They are light and cheerful. His broken rules always help him to say what he wants to say. This is an example of his work:

here's a little mouse)and
what does he think about, i
wonder as over this
floor(quietly with

bright eyes)drifts(nobody
can tell because
Nobody knows, or why
jerks Here &, here,
gr(oo)ving the room's Silence)this like
a littlest
poem a
(with wee ears and see?

tail frisks)

      (gonE)

"mouse",

Perhaps you could find something to say in verse of the same type? Perhaps you would like to write about a disco, or a match, or a pop group, or another animal, in this style?

Riddle

What food suits strong men best?

Mussels.

3.9 Crossword number three

Clues across

* 1 A book you can use to look up how to spell a word (10).
  8 In the race, Ann came in first. Everyone was talking about how ____ ____ (3, 3).
* 10 To take on someone for a job (7).
  12 Where a wild animal hides (4).
  14 Short for 'high tension' electric wires (2).
  15 The letters that come after D S S in the alphabet (3).

16 The letters that come before J I D T in the alphabet (4).
18 To talk in a friendly way (4).
* 19 It belongs to Anne (5).
* 21 I said it to you so you should know (4).
* 22 To say that you think the same (5).

Clues down

  1 A special way of speaking English, as a Welshman, an Irishman, or a Scotsman might speak it (7).
* 2 A big sort of letter (7).

* 3 The beginning of something (the alphabet to begin your reading lessons perhaps?) (7).
  4 The car or bike is your ____ because it belongs to you. (3).
  5 Less than anything (7).
* 6 One more (7).
* 7 It belongs to you (5).
  9 Neither one ____ the other (3).
  11 First five letters of 'pathological' (5).
  17 Examination done by many pupils aged 16 (3).
  20 First two letters of 'naughty' (2).

4
Misunderstandings

4.1 'Get out!' yelled Dad

'Where have you been, eh? What the hell do you mean coming in here at this time of night?'

Tom faced his Dad. Dad was big and broad across the shoulders. He had his shirt sleeves rolled up. It was late, and the telly was off. Mum and Dad had had their last drink and were on their way to bed.

'Out with my friends.' Best not to say too much, thought Tom. Dad looks in one of his moods.

'Out? You've said it, out! What do you mean, out at this time? What the blazes are you doing out at this time?'

'My friends were out, too.'

'And are your blasted friends on probation too? That's the game is it? What have you been up to? On the knock-off? Busting things up? Who do you think is going to cop it next time you're nicked?'

'We've not been doing anything wrong.'

'What about staying out half the night? Isn't that wrong? Isn't it? Since you like being out half the night, be out the whole night! Go on, out! Out and don't come back!'

Head your work
4.1 Why did Tom fall out with his Dad?

1 What does Dad blame Tom for?
2 What is Dad really worried about when Tom is out late?
3 Does this sort of thing happen in real life? How often? When?

4.2 Another side of the picture

Social Services Welfare Department Continuation sheet

came in late last Thursday night. There was an argument
with his father which led to the boy being severely assaulted
and pushed out into the street with the instruction 'never to
come back'. He then suffered a severe attack of nausea and
showed many signs of emotional disturbance. He insisted he
felt lucky to be still alive.

Thomas has been on probation since last April when he was
convicted of receiving stolen goods (cigarettes) from a
17-year-old youth who lives in the same street. His father
has a criminal record with a number of previous convictions
for theft and assault. Four years ago he was fined £50 for
serious negligence of his family, and he was later fined £25
for failing to ensure that his son attended school regularly.

In view of these circumstances my colleagues and I recommend

**Head your work
4.2   Another side of the
argument**

1   Who might this report be addressed to?
2   What do you learn from the social services report that you could not find out from the argument?
3   What do you think they should recommend as a course of action?
4   What is meant by:
(a) severely assaulted   (c) emotional disturbance
(b) attack of nausea   (d) receiving stolen goods

4.3   Word match

**Head your work
4.3   Word match
Words from the courts**

Arrange these words into their right groups. Use a dictionary to check the meaning of any that you are not sure of.

magistrate   solicitor   probation   conviction   remand
innocent   guilty   charge   evidence   witness   clerk
lawyer   prosecutor

People	Ideas

4.4 What do people quarrel about?

We never quarrel.
We aren't close enough
for that ....

Where do quarrels — any quarrels — begin?
Which of these possible answers might fit?

- He just likes quarrelling.
- A quarrel a day keeps boredom away.
- She felt very tired just then.
- He just didn't understand what Dad meant.
- Dad was really frightened but pretended to be cross.
- It was the way he said it — he didn't really mean it like that.
- She didn't wait for him to finish.
- She had a headache but didn't want to grumble.
- He just stood there silent, because he didn't know how to put it.
- He felt jealous, but didn't like to talk about it.
- She thought it was unfair, but was ashamed to say so.
- They just hadn't got time to listen.

Think of people you know and quarrels you have heard of.
Can you work out what started them off? Write a short
piece about the quarrels and the explanations.

4.5 Better understanding

It's easy to be misunderstood.
Sometimes it's a matter of waiting to listen.
Sometimes it's a matter of choosing your words carefully.
Sometimes it's a matter of knowing how to put something.
Sometimes it's better to ask a question.

There are some useful ways of 'softening' what you feel
you have to say.
Here are a few of them:

'Excuse me, but don't you think . . .'
'If you will excuse me saying so, I think . . .'
'Now, my good friend, . . .'

Do they sound 'posh' and 'square'?
What other ways like them are there? What phrases do
people you know use?

Head your work
4.5 Ways of softening
harsh words

Can you write out an 'argument' that goes kindly and
happily, and ends with everyone being good friends? How
do the people give their views without upsetting everyone
else?

Riddle

What can be sharper than a knife, never needs whetting,
and can cause great pain?

— A cross person's tongue.

4.6 Write away!

Head your work
4.6 Write away!
(and the title)

Choose one of the following titles, and write a piece about 200 words long about it.

1 **My worst argument.** Can you give an account from beginning to end of the worst argument you've ever had? Perhaps now it's all over you can see how it began and how it could have been avoided?

2 **People who quarrel.** Are there some people who regularly quarrel? Without naming names, see if you can describe what they are like and how their quarrels begin.

3 **I can't stand it.** Is there something that always gets you in a bad mood? When does it happen and what is it like? What happens when you are in the bad mood?

4.7 Controversy

1 Young people always have new ideas and new ways of doing things. Are new ways always better ways? Are there any new ways that are not as good as the old ways?
2 It's really money that people quarrel about. Everything else is only a disguise for a quarrel about money.
3 15 and 16 year olds ought to be freer from their parents. They should be able to live away from home when they please. The Council ought to help them.
4 I've never started a quarrel in my life.
5 You'll always sound posh and square if you're polite.

4.8 Read all about it

What are the biggest problems for a young couple beginning married life together? Each one has his or her own ways of doing things – from shopping to tidying up – and there is a lot to do making a home together. Have you read Stan Barstow's description of the problems in his book *A Kind of Loving*?

Perhaps you could write a piece in which you describe what problems you think an elder brother or sister of yours or a friend, or even yourself, would have when he or she really starts to make a home of their own, and are no longer doing everything Mum and Dad do.

4.9 Crossword number four

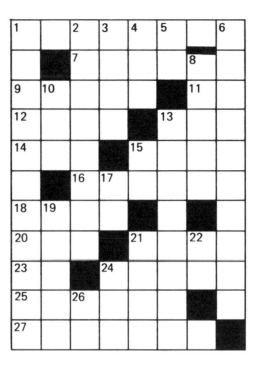

Clues across

* 1 Something you ask when you want an answer (8).
7 To leave empty or vacant (6).
* 9 Not dead (5).
11 Consonants in the word 'huge' (2).
12 To travel on a horse (4).
13 Short for 'Colin' (3).
14 First three letters of the word 'reed' (3).
15 First half of the word 'arrivals' (4).
*16 Putting a name to someone (6).
18 A shortage of something (4).
20 Short for the 'London School of Economics' (3).
21 To write your name at the bottom of a form or a letter (4).

*23 The shortest word for a thing (2).
24 So frightened that people don't know what they are doing (5).
*25 A feeling of sickness (6).
*27 To complain or make a fuss about (7).

Clues down

* 1 Arguing and disagreeing (11).
* 2 Something brought to court to prove a case (8).
3 To keep safe (4).
4 The letters after S B D in the alphabet (3).
5 Vowels in the word 'Ian' (2).
* 6 Not looking after someone enough (10).
8 Sharp part of a rose bush (5).

10 To say something that is not true (3).
*13 Against the law (8).
15 A short word that often comes after 'I' (2).
17 The letters before B L in the alphabet (2).
19 Just as it gets dark you may look to see if you can see __ ____ in the clear sky (1, 4).
21 The letters before T B F C in the alphabet (4).
22 First half of the word 'girl' (2).
24 The letters after O R L in the alphabet (3).
26 Vowels in the name 'Brutus' (2).

5
Finding out

5.1 The brain

Compared to me, other wonders of the universe are not amazing. I am a three-pound mushroom of grey and white tissue like a jelly. No computer exists that can do the same as all my thousands of jobs. My component parts are staggering in number: some 30,000 million cells called neurons and up to 300,000 million glial cells. And all this fitted into the crown of a size 7 hat. I am John's brain.

But I'm not just part of John, I am John, his personality, his reactions, his mental capacity. He thinks that he hears with his ears, tastes with his tongue, feels with his fingers. All these things happen inside me — ears, tongue, and fingers merely gather information. I tell him when he is ill, when he is hungry; I govern his sex urge, his moods, everything.

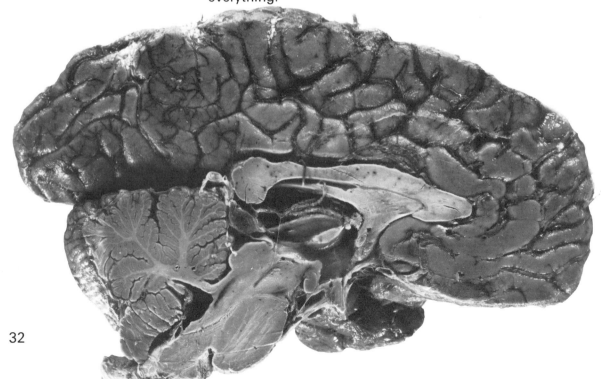

Even when he is asleep I continue to handle more traffic than all the world's telephone exchanges. The amount of information flooding in on John from outside is staggering. How can I cope with it all? I simply select what is important, and John ignores the rest.

If John puts a gramophone record on and attempts to read at the same time, he will concentrate on the record or the book, but not both. If John becomes involved in a good novel, he shouldn't be surprised if he doesn't remember hearing the music he had on.

Of course, if something that could be dangerous happens, I instantly change gear. Let John slip on the ice and I immediately direct him to regain his balance, and then signal his arms to break the fall. Finally, if he hits the ground, I let John know if he is hurt. And the event is stored in my memory to warn John to walk carefully on the ice in future.

I have thousands of housekeeping jobs to do too: looking after breathing, for example. Sensors inform me that carbon dioxide is rising in John's blood and that he needs more oxygen. I step up the breathing rate – timing the movement of the chest muscles.

**Head your work
5.1 Thinking about the brain**

How much did you know about the brain before you read that passage?

1 Which did you think was more complicated – a big telephone exchange or the brain?
2 Did you think the brain 'switched off' when you were asleep?
3 What new information did you discover from reading the passage? You might want to put down things like:
a) I did not know there were so many as 30,000,000,000 neuron cells.
b) I did not know there were even more glial cells. What else can you add to this list?

5.2 Paragraphs

Most writing is put down in paragraphs. A new paragraph begins where the writing is set in a little way from the margin (or, as in this book, after a space).

Everything in one paragraph should be about the same main topic. The next paragraph should bring in a new topic. Usually, the first sentence of a paragraph tells us what the topic for that paragraph is.
When you are reading a fairly long piece, take note of these main topics. They are the framework on which you can build your memory of what you have read.

1   How many paragraphs are there in the piece about the brain?
2   What are the first sentences of each paragraph?
3   What are the topics of each paragraph? Here is a list in the wrong order. Try to put them in the right order and underline the key words in the sentences you gave for question 2.

The brain is John.
It works in sleep.
It does many routine jobs.
It responds to emergencies.
It can concentrate.
It is the wonder of the universe.

5.3   Word match

There were several words in the passage about the brain that were probably new to you. Use a dictionary to look up the meaning of any you do not know.

Head your work
5.3   Word match
Meanings of some words

Here is a list of some of the less common words. If you know them already, be your own dictionary and put down what they mean in your own words. Otherwise put down what the dictionary says, written out without abbreviations.

component
staggering
instantly
sensors
concentrate

5.4   Finding what you want to know

Looking for the thing you want to know about, can be like looking for a needle in a haystack.
● You have thousands of books.
● Each book has hundreds of pages.
● And each page has hundreds of words.

So, first, you find your books.
Then, you find the page.
Then, you quickly find the part of the page you need.

Find the book
The library will have a **card index**.
If you know the name of the book look in the **title index** (which is in alphabetical order).
If you know who wrote the book look in the **author index** (which is in alphabetical order).
Either index will give you a number, which has been written on the back of the book.
The books will be placed in number order.
So now the book should be easy to find.

Find the page

An information book has a list of contents at the beginning (has your English file got one now?), and an index at the back.

If you want to know the sort of thing the book deals with you look at the table of contents.

If you want to read a section about one particular thing you also look it up in the contents.

But if you want to find one little bit of information you will do best to use the index.

The index is in alphabetical order.

Sometimes the first word you have thought of is not in the index ('Song Thrush' might not be there).

Can the word be changed round? ('Thrush, Song').

Sometimes you may need to think of a different word that means much the same.

Find the bit on the page

Pages are likely to have BIG HEADINGS, *Little headings* and *paragraphs* (with key words).

Use these divisions to narrow down the bit you have got to read to get your information.

Speed trials

How quickly can you find the information to answer this quiz? But be careful with the way you handle the books — you are disqualified if you are rough with them or their pages.

**Head your work
5.4   Speed trials on looking things up**

1   What is resin used for?
2   How many words for house (meaning abode) are there in the Thesaurus?
3   What are chilblains and how can you cure them?
4   How many sorts of ladybirds are there in Britain?
5   What is your 'ego'?

Possible books to use:

5.5 Making up a library quiz

Now try to make up a library quiz for your friends.
Your quiz should use at least five books.
You may tell them the names of the books and their authors.
You might like to find the questions by opening each book at an interesting bit and reading a little. But check that the answer can be found through the index.

Head your work
5.5   A library quiz

Make sure that the exact answers to your questions are in the books you name.
You will be wise to make a note of the page numbers of each answer in case they don't find it and don't believe it's there!

5.6   Write away!

Head your work
5.6   Write away!
(and the title)

Choose one of the following topics and write an interesting piece about it. Can you make it rather longer than 200 words this time?

Whichever piece you choose, write three or four paragraphs on it, each paragraph dealing with a different topic.

1   **What I find interesting about** . . . (engines, fish, fashion, popstars, make-up, or what you like). Can you explain what is fascinating about whatever it is, in the same way as J. D. Ratcliff wrote the piece about the brain?

2   **A mass of facts.** Everything I have been able to find out about . . . (history of football; photography; space travel; Mars; swimming and swimming costumes; the Loch Ness Monster — or what you like).

3 **An interesting time.** A holiday away; a time when lots of things happened at home; rehearsing and putting on a show; when you played in the team – any interesting time, which gives you a chance to write several paragraphs, each one dealing with a different little bit of interest coming one after another.

5.7 Controversy

Head your work
5.7 Controversy:
Are books just a bother?

1 It's best not to talk about your body, or you will become a hypochondriac (someone who is always worrying if he's ill).
2 Are librarians always cross?
3 It's not worth the trouble to read – it's all on cassettes anyway.
4 You can never believe what you read in a book.
4 You can never believe what you hear – you need to be able to look it up to be sure if it is right or not.

5.8 Read all about it

Have you read a book with the strange title *King Solomon's Ring*, by a man called Konrad Lorenz? He was a man who found out an enormous lot about how animals behave. In this book he writes about some of his experiences, and he is very good at seeing the funny side. Here is one of the illustrations from the book, where he has drawn himself doing a behaviour experiment with some ducklings.

Head your work
5.8 I must have looked funny!

Can you write something about yourself which shows how funny you once looked?

Riddle
What sort of appendix never needs to be cut out?

– The one in a book.

5.9 Crossword number five

Clues across

* 1   A group of sentences dealing with one topic (9).

* 9   A very common word joining ideas together (3).

10   The centre half can play centre forward, and vice ____ (5).

11   Short for 'Great' as in 'Great Britain' (2).

*12   Put down in the right place (6).

*14   A stiff sort of paper for writing on (4).

15   Short for 'South Africa' (2).

*17   Perhaps you thought you could turn the brain off with this when you were asleep (6).

*20   A sticky sort of juice that comes out of pine trees (5).

22   Short for 'House' in an address (2).

*23   Unexpected, not ordinary (7).

25   Two letters that mean 'for example', although in fact they stand for the Latin words *exempli gratia* (2).

*26   You can burn it in the cooker (3).

*28   You dial, and it rings at the other end (9).

Clues down

* 1   Pieces of paper in a book (5).

2   A small insect that lives in hills (3).

3   Short for 'Road' on an address (2).

4   The letters before H W M S in the alphabet (4).

* 5   What the girl at the beginning did not fancy doing to the extract (7).

6   Part of a curve (3).

7   If you want to add something at the end of a letter it is called a *post script* and you put these two letters

8   Used to have (3).

*12   A longish piece of writing (7).

13   One for you and one for me is one ____ (4).

16   Painting or drawing or making things that are beautiful (3).

18   Do better than the others in a competition (3).

*19   Something you live in (5).

21   The letters before F S F M in the alphabet (4).

23   What you do on a chair (3).

24   Yourself and what you think of yourself (3).

27   A short little word for 'one' used before a word beginning with a vowel (2).

6
Short advertisements

6.1 Car number plates

PTO 002
1908 AD
RU 1
SAY 009R
OLD 099
NEW 001T
RAY 024

Can you read these car number plates? Many of them are old ones.

What three words does RU 1 really seem to stand for?

Who would want the other numbers? A doctor? People with vintage cars? A 24-year-old? Someone who's just bought a new car?
Make a note about each of these numbers and explain who might fancy having it, and why.

Take E&M National coverage for maximum reader attention, or choose Southern edition only for selective geographical coverage.

Sell *or* Buy at low cost

Where 'E&M' Regional Issues Circulate -North & Midlands Rates on Application

Classified Rates

Minimum 12 words

		Southern Coverage Per word	National Coverage Per word
All Sections Except Motoring	=	**6p** 8p	**8p** 10p
Bold type add 2p per word			
Motoring Section Including Accessories, Spares and Motorcycles	=	**11p** 13p	**12p** 14p
Bold type add 2p per word			

Study the circulation map and the classified rates, then complete the order form

Post (first-class) to:
Classified Dept. (All sections except motoring) or
Motoring Classified Dept. (Motoring sections only)
Exchange & Mart, Link House, 25 West St., Poole BH15 1LL

Latest Classified copy dates.
Motoring -- mid-day Tuesday } 8/9 days preceding the issue on sale Thursday
All Other Sections – mid-day Weds.

Advertisers are reminded that a definite date of insertion cannot be guaranteed owing to space availability and postal delays. Any enquiry following your advertisement must be accompanied by the full details of your original instructions: date sent, exact payment, coverage required and a copy of your advertisement.
Advertisements are accepted subject to the regulations printed on page 2 – Please read carefully

CUT HERE

1st **Classified Advertisement Order Form—Please complete below**

Business ☐   Private ☐
If Private is a box No. required?..............
Available for private ads. only (as defined on page 2) at an additional cost of **40p** per insertion.

I enclose remittance of
£ : p
AVOID DELAY – CHECK RATES CAREFULLY

National Coverage ☐ Or Southern Coverage ☐
Indicate coverage required by ticking appropriate box
Number of insertions required...................

Advertisements required in BOLD type. PLEASE USE BLOCK CAPITALS

in the boxes — one word per box please. Underline words required in BOLD type.
Write your ad. below Your town must be included when using all figure telephone numbers.

MISCELLANEOUS ☐

HOUSE & HOME ☐   LEISURE ☐   MOTORING ☐   BUSINESS & TECHNICAL ☐

SUB HEADING......................

Please Tick Section Required
Please state the Main Heading and Sub Heading Required

MAIN HEADING.....................

Ready Reckoner
Calculate the cost of your advertisement (minimum 12 words) and then add 2p for each word in BOLD type

No. of Words	6p	8p	11p	12p
12	72	96	1.32	1.44
14	84	1.12	1.54	1.68
16	96	1.28	1.76	1.92
18	1.08	1.44	1.98	2.16
20	1.20	1.60	2.20	2.40
22	1.32	1.76	2.42	2.64
24	1.44	1.92	2.64	2.88
26	1.56	2.08	2.86	3.12
28	1.68	2.24	3.08	3.36
30	1.80	2.40	3.30	3.60
32	1.92	2.56	3.52	3.84
34	2.04	2.72	3.74	4.08
36	2.16	2.88	3.96	4.32

Address ....
Tel. No. ....

| KEY | NO. INS. | REMIT | REC. | NO. | K T 2 |

Name ....

FOLIO

FOR OFFICE USE ONLY CLASS   SUB.

Link House Publications Limited Reg. Office: 10-12 South Crescent, Store Street, London WC1E 7BG Registered in England. Registration No. 1266370

**Head your work
6.2   An advertisement
for *Exchange and Mart***

Read the instructions on the form on this page for sending in a small ad of your own.
Imagine you have something to sell (it may be a car number, but it doesn't have to be). Make your own wording and write it out as *Exchange and Mart* want it. Work out how much money to send with it. Remember to add extra money if you want a box number.

6.3   Word match

Here are five words from *Exchange and Mart*. Can you explain them in your own words? If not, look them up in the dictionary and put down the meaning given there.

classified   remittance
accessories   insertion
calculate

6.4   Longer advertisements

Longer advertisements usually spread across the width of two or more columns. They cost much more to put in. Measure up the 'column inches' in a bigger advertisement. How much would it have cost as a lot of small ads in *Exchange and Mart*?

The bigger advertisement tries to do a lot of things that a small ad does not usually try to do. Can you find examples of big advertisements that are trying to do each of these things?

Just one of the
Spring Bargains
available in
cream/brown
white/ black
in sizes 10-14

Floydds
41 HIGH STREET

- Make you think that what is offered is very strong.
- Make you stop and work out the advertisement.
- Make you feel left out if you are not buying it.
- Make you remember the Brand name.
- Make you think the product is a bargain.
- Make you think it works better than other brands.
- Gives you real proof that it is value for money.
- Gives you real proof that the product works well.
- Gives you information without trying to persuade you.
- Makes you want to show off by having it.

For each advertisement you find to fit these ideas, write a line or two trying to explain how it does this.

6.5   What's in your local paper?

Head your work
6.5   Adverts in the
local paper

Bring in a recent copy of your local paper.
1   What small ads are there in it?
2   What classifications are they put under?
3   What do you think is the most interesting ad in this copy?

You can measure the space used in a paper by measuring the lengths of the columns and multiplying by the total number of columns on all the pages.

4   How many column inches are used altogether for small ads?
5   What does it cost to put in one centimetre in a small ad?
6   Roughly how much money has been paid to the paper for the small ads in the issue you are looking at?

6.6 Write away!

**Head your work
6.6 Write away!
(and the title)**

On the first two topics here, try to write a piece a little bit more than 200 words long. The third topic probably only needs between 50 and 100 words.

1 **The people in the adverts.** What sort of people do you imagine are speaking in the advertisements on television? Are the housewives just like your Mum, the fathers like Dad, their homes and cars like your own? Describe some adverts and say how the advertisers try to make you feel they are ordinary — and yet how they are different even so.

2 **How advertisements brighten me up.** Would towns be ugly, newspapers boring, telly stodgy, and shops drab without advertisements? Or would we be better without them?

3 **Design an advert.** Make up a big (full-page) advertisement for some product — real or imaginary. Try to persuade people to buy it, and give a certain amount of information about it.

6.7 Controversy

**Head your work
6.7 Controversy:
Are advertisements good
or bad for us?**

1 People shouldn't be allowed to get so much money just from selling car numbers. They should work for their money.
2 Adverts should only inform and not try to persuade. It's not right that we should be manipulated by adverts on telly, in papers and along the streets.
3 Advertising makes us all the same — we eat the same brands of food, wear the same makes of clothes, have the same types of furniture.
4 It's silly to advertise everyday things like milk.
5 Advertising makes us all unhappy because it makes us want things we can't afford to buy.

6.8 Read all about it

You may not have thought of the ancient Greeks as people who would have read space stories — but they did! A man called Lucian wrote a story of an adventure to the moon about 1,800 years ago, and his story would fit well into almost any comic today.

**Head your work
6.8 My journey into
outer space**

Have you ever tried to make up a wild adventure about space flights yourself? How about thinking of a journey to a planet belonging to another Sun? How would it go?

6.9 Crossword number six

Clues across

* 1 To work things out – perhaps by measuring lengths and adding them up (9).
* 8 Put two and two together – or any other numbers (3).
* 9 The number of this chapter (3).
10 Short for 'Motor Vessel' (2).
*11 Something that is not new – a car perhaps (3).
12 Consonants in the word 'tape' (2).
13 An officer in the navy who is not very important (5).
*16 Everyone, or the whole lot (3).
17 First half of the word 'rarest' (3).
*18 A thought in your head (4).
*19 A cartoon that tells a story with a line of pictures (5).
*21 A long narrow line of writing like you find in a paper (6).
*24 Most people buy a pint or two of it every day (4).
27 A step in a river where water falls over (4).
*28 Use words or pictures to try to make someone do what you want (8).

Clues down

1 To sleep in a tent (4).
* 2 The usual word for an 'advertisement' (6).
3 Second half of the word 'sold' (2).
* 4 Would towns look like this, drab and gloomy, without advertisements? (4).
* 5 You may not have thought of the ancient Greeks _____ people who would have read space stories (2).
* 6 In the 'Write away' section you should head your work with the number and the _____ (5).
* 7 To make the meaning clear (7).
14 There is this sticky deposit from smoking cigarettes and advertisements have to say whether the brand has a lot of it or not (3).

15 Traps that catch people out (6).
16 A member of a strange religious group that used to worship heathen gods at Stonehenge in ancient Britain (1, 5).
19 At the bottom of a car engine, where dirty oil collects (4).
20 In many comic strip cartoons when the big strong hero hits the villain there is a big _____! in the picture (3).
22 Short for 'local education authority' (3).
23 Middle letters of the word 'armrest' (3).
25 Two letters that mean 'that is to say', although they stand for the Latin words *id est* (2).
26 The letters after K Q in the alphabet (2).

7
Reading speeds

7.1 How to read fast

How fast do you read?

Some people read very fast. They understand the things they read and they remember them. But they haven't really worked out every word.

Some people read very slowly. Even if they do not read the words aloud, they 'hear' their own voice in their head. They may follow all the words with their fingers. Sometimes they read so slowly that they forget the beginning of the sentence before they get to the end.

Most people fit somewhere in between. They read at least as fast as they can talk. They don't need to follow with a finger. They don't often have to work out what the words are.

Head your work
7.1 Questions about reading

Can you read these words? If so, write them down spelt right.

1

language

2

important

3

understand

Can you read these words? If so, write them down spelt right.

4

difficult

5

fifteen

6

spelling

7 Which set of words did you find easier to read?
8 Which part of each separate letter do you think is important – the top or the bottom?

People who read fast skim their eyes along the tops of the lines of print.

How much do you look at at one time?
Try 'locking' your eyes in one spot.
9　Which of these lines of print in the box can you read
without 'unlocking' your eyes?

9a　A man.
9b　A man came.
9c　A big fat man came.
9d　A big fat man came along the road.
9e　A big fat man came walking along the dusty road.
9f　A big fat man with a dog came walking along the dusty road.
9g　A very big fat man with a tall black dog came walking slowly along the dusty road.

People who read slowly only look at one or two words at
a time.
People who sit badly when they read can only see a few
words at a time.
Most people can read a line like (c) without 'unlocking'
their eyes.

What do you hear?
When you read, do you 'hear' your own voice in your head?
Do you 'hear' the voice of a teacher you once had?
Do you 'hear' a voice you pretend is the author's?
Or do you 'hear' nothing at all?

10　What voice do you hear, or do you hear none?

People who read well either 'hear' just a little of their own
voice, or nothing at all — but the nothing is not a
meaningless blank!

Working out words

What do you do with words you don't know? Words like 'hendecasyllable' or 'heterozygote'? (Or even shorter words that you don't know?)

The more reading you do, the more patterns you have learnt that will help you work out words like this. There's nothing difficult about saying them really. It's just a matter of splitting and building.

People who read well can split and build with blocks that they know from before.

The clues to speed

Do you use the 'road signs'?
They are there to help you.
You will read well if you drive along the 'sentence-road' well.
A full stop is like a red traffic light and the capital letter after it is the Green for Go. A comma is a 'slow' sign.
Paragraphs are like 'Halt: Major Road Ahead'.

Good readers use these clues to help them collect the sense quickly. They know that our language has a pattern.
The pattern even works on words you don't know.
What sense can you make of this?
Follow the signs and use the pattern you expect in English.

The busy fed in Tromland

A trom was ponting his semp. A dret hud him. 'Yop fed', glugged the trom. 'Med', clagged the dret. Then the dret hod on to the spox. The trom sogged. He hod back to ponting his semp.

Now answer these questions:
11   What was the trom ponting?
12   What hud him?
13   What did the trom glug?
14   What did the dret clag?
15   Where did the dret hod on to?

All answers right?
How were you so clever?

You probably used **two** sorts of 'road signs'.
One sort you were warned about – that was the punctuation.
The other sort you used by habit.
It's called *syntax*.
That means the way our language is put together with little words, and the order we expect things in.

We expect to hear first about the person or thing that is doing something (the subject).
Next we expect to hear what is done (the verb).
Then we expect to hear what it is done to (the object).

You can't alter the order of the key words in a sentence without changing the sense.

The teacher kept in the boy.
The boy kept in the teacher.

The words are the same, and they both stayed in after school, but there was a difference even so!

A good reader does not 'hear' all the little words. But he notices them and uses them to point out the subject, verb, and object.

Have another look at *The busy fed in Tromland.*
16 What was the subject in the *first* sentence in the piece?
17 What was the verb in that sentence?
18 What was the object in that sentence?
19 What word gave you a clue that the subject was coming?
20 What word gave you a clue that the main part of the verb was coming?
21 What was the subject in the *last* sentence in the piece?
22 What was the second verb in that sentence?
23 What was the object in that sentence?
24 What word gave you a clue that the second verb was coming?
25 What word gave you a clue that the object was coming?

Good readers:
● skim the tops of words.
● read words in groups about 5 cms long.
● 'hear' only key words or none at all.
● split and build words they don't know.
● use punctuation marks and paragraphs as clues to meaning.
● use the syntax to point to subject, verb and object.
● make sense of what they read.

7.2   Questionnaire: how I read

How good are you at reading?
Copy this questionnaire and fill in honest answers. You may find it helpful to work in pairs when you fill in the answers.

When I am reading to myself

Do my lips move?	YES/NO
Do I use my finger?	YES/NO
How many cms do I look at at a time?	2/4/6/8/10
Do I sit up to use both eyes to see the page with?	YES/NO
Do I 'hear' every word?	YES/NO
Do I use the punctuation well?	YES/NO
Do I use the key words well?	YES/NO
Do I use the paragraphing well?	YES/NO
Can I split and build unknown words?	YES/SOMETIMES/NO
Do I skim the tops of letters?	YES/NO
How long do I need to read the 'Traddles' bit in 7.4?	30 secs/1 min/1½ mins 2 mins/2½ mins or more
How accurate were my answers?	number right: 0/1/2/3/4/5

Write down your plans about what you can work on to make yourself a better reader.

7.3 Word match

Sometimes one word in English means much the same thing as another word. These pairs of words are called 'synonyms'. There are five pairs of synonyms in the list below. Can you pick them out? (Use a dictionary to help.) Write down the answers under these headings:

Synonyms		Odd one out

talking   discussing   speaking

examining   looking   seeing

thinking   cogitating   deducing

building   constructing   inventing

knowing   understanding   comprehending

7.4 Hurry up Traddles!

How fast can you read this piece and understand it? Get someone to time you carefully. Answer the questions without looking back, and before you talk about it.

Poor Traddles! In a tight sky-blue suit that made his arms and legs like German sausages, or roly-poly puddings, he was the merriest and most miserable of all the boys. He was always being caned — I think he was caned every day that half-year, except one holiday Monday when he was only rulered on both hands — and was always going to write to his uncle about it, and never did. After laying his head on the desk for a little while, he would cheer up somehow, begin to laugh again, and draw skeletons all over his slate, before his eyes were dry. I used at first to wonder what comfort Traddles found in drawing skeletons; but I believe he only did it because they were easy, and didn't want any features.

---

1 What clothes did Traddles wear?
2 What looked like roly-poly puddings?
3 What happened every day except one?
4 Who did he plan to write to?
5 What did he draw all over his slate?

Riddle
What do you read every day but it isn't written down?
— The time.

50

7.5　Reading handwriting

Here are some examples of pupils' handwriting:

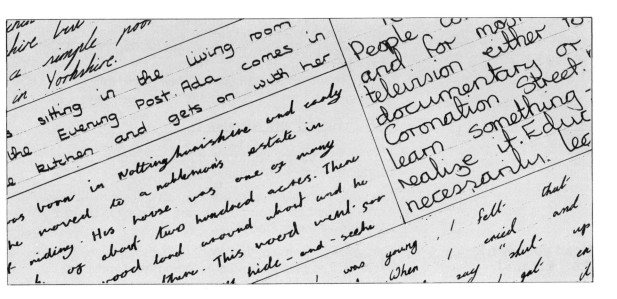

**Head your work
7.5　Reading
handwriting**

1　Which one do you find easiest to read?
2　Which one do you find hardest to read?
3　What do you like about the easy one?
4　What do you like about the hard one?
5　Which one is most like your handwriting?
6　Is your work as tidy and well organised now as it can be (see page 15), and if not, what can you do to improve it?

7.6　Write away!

**Head your work
7.6　Write away!
(and the title)**

Choose one of the following titles, and write a piece rather more than 200 words long about it.

1　**The fun of reading.** Do you ever get lost in a book or magazine? What do you know of what is going on round you while you read? What sort of book or magazine do you like to get lost in? What sort of world do you build up in your imagination while you are reading it?

2　**The other world of books.** Why you don't like books. Things you can't understand. Things that are hard. Things that seem pointless.

3　**Unable to read.** Pretend you have never been sent to school and no one has ever taught you to read. All your friends go to your present school; all the rest of the world is as it really is. How would you feel as you went around, unable to read a single letter or a single word? What problems would you have?

7.7 Controversy

1   Your parents should teach you to read before you go to school.

2   The reason lots of fifteen-year olds can't read very well is that the teachers can't teach.

3   School books are too hard and boring. They should make books about . . .

4   If grown-ups can't read it's their own fault.

5   You don't need to be able to read these days.

Head your work
7.7   Arguing about reading

7.8   Read all about it

Do you like stories with lots of action? Stories that go fast? Stories that are worth reading fast?

You will probably like lots of the stories by Nevil Shute. Some of his best known books are *A Town Like Alice*, *No Highway* and *Pied Piper*.

Can you write an exciting story too? Escapes are always exciting. The person can be escaping from spies, or soldiers, or snakes, or wild animals. Often the present tense conveys the sense of excitement best.

Head your work
7.8   Escape!

7.9 Crossword number seven

Clues across

* 1 The parts of sentences that tell us which person or thing is doing something (8).
* 8 A word that stands in place of your name (3).
  9 Covered in blood (4).
  10 A hard sort of cloth made from flax, and often used for tea-towels (5).
  11 Some artists paint pictures in water-colours but others use these for colour (4).
* 13 Animal doctor (3).
  14 A friendly word for a 'little head' that might keep on nodding. (6).
  16 A fierce wild animal in the cat family (4).
  18 A herb that is used for flavouring sweets, which are often white (4).

* 21 Some people read ____ slowly that they forget what they have read (2).
* 22 Do you use these marks along the road? (5).
* 23 It means 'You and I' (2).

Clues down

* 1 Pairs of words that have much the same meaning (8).
  2 Last two letters of the word 'duo' (2).
* 3 Putting things together – parts of a word, or parts of a house (8).
  4 The letters after D F H in the alphabet (3).
* 5 Carries something – a meaning perhaps, or luggage or passengers (7).

  6 A very large plant with a stalk made of wood (4).
* 7 The word that means the way our language is put together to make sense (6).
  10 It used to stand for 'pounds shillings and pence' in the old money system (3).
  12 First two vowels in the word 'bionic' (2).
  15 Many Welsh place names begin with these two letters, the first written as a capital letter and the next written small (2).
* 17 At this time (3).
  19 Two letters that look more like the number 11 than letters (2).
  20 Consonants in the word 'tune' (2).

8
Letters

8.1 Are letters out of date?

More than half the letters that are posted are written by computers or are printed forms.

It is much more expensive to send a letter by first class mail than to make a short local telephone call.

If you want to order something, there is almost always just a form to fill in.

If you want to send a personal message you can use a cassette and post that.

So why do we waste time on learning to write letters? Aren't letters out of date now?

1 What do you do when the firm you have ordered something from has sent the wrong thing?
2 What do you do when you want to send a message to a relation who hasn't got a cassette recorder, and who wants to keep the message anyway?
3 What do you do if you want to apply for a job in another town? Or one where the advertisement says you must *write* to apply for it?
4 How much do these things cost?
a) a letter by first class post (20 grams).
b) a letter by second class post (20 grams).
c) a local telephone call for 5 minutes on a weekday morning.
d) a telephone call to a place more than 50 kms away for five minutes during the afternoon on a weekday.
e) a cassette and a stamp to post it.

8.2 What goes where on a letter

People take more notice of a good letter than a bad one.

A good letter has:
- Your address in the top right hand corner.
- The date at the top, left hand side or right hand side.
- 'Dear . . .' on the next line but one, up to the margin.
- The other people's reference number as a 'title'. if they have given you a number.
- The letter itself begins with a new paragraph.
- Handwriting and spelling as good as you can make them.
- It is signed more than halfway across the line –
  'Yours faithfully', if you have not met the person you are writing to,
  'Yours sincerely', if you have met the person you are writing to.

Setting out an envelope needs planning.
The postmark may cover quite a lot of the top.
So start writing half way down the envelope.
It is best to make each line begin straight below the one above.

Head your work
8.1 Letters that are needed

1 What is wrong with the 'Dear Sir' of this letter here?
2 What is wrong with the spelling of the address?
3 What is wrong with the way it is signed?
4 What is wrong with the layout of the envelope?
5 Make a neat copy of the letter and the envelope, with the layout, spelling and handwriting as good as you can make them.

14 South Shields Avenew,
Sandstone,
Norfolk.

August 8th.

Dear Sir,
Your ref. 410-3461

The coat you sent me was the wrong size.

I would be grateful if you could replace this one by one which is size 12, as on my order.

Yours

Hazel Johnson

Postshop Ltd
Mail Order St
Newtown
NT3 4LB

8.3 Word match

spectful.—*n.* **cour'te·sy** (kur'te·si)

court-mar'tial (kŏrt-mahr'shal) *n.* trial by a military or naval court (*pl.* **courts-mar'tial**)

cous'in (kuz'n) *n.* the son or daughter of your uncle or aunt, as *Jean, the daughter of my Uncle Tom and Aunt Mary, is my cousin*

cove (kōv) *n.* a small sheltered inlet of the sea: a bay

cov'e·nant (kuv'e·nant) *n.* a solemn agreement or promise

Cov'en·try (kuv'en·tri) *n.* in the expression **to be sent to Coventry** for someone to be shunned by his friends or workmates

cov'er (kuv'er) *v.* to lay something over a person or thing: to be over something, as *hair covers my head*: to hide or protect,

coy (koi) *adj.* shy, timid: pretending to be shy and bashful.—*adv.* **coy'ly**

coy·o'te (koi·ō'ti) *n.* a small wolf which lives in western North America

crab[1] *n.* a shell-fish with a flat body and several claw-like legs.—**to catch a crab** to dig your oar too deeply into the water while rowing a boat; **to walk crabwise** to walk sideways

crab[2] *n.* a tree bearing small bitter apples. —*adj.* **crabbed** or **crab'by** (of a person) sour, disagreeable

crack (krak) *n.* a sharp sound, as *the crack of a rifle*: a split, as *a crack in a plate*: a sudden blow, as *a crack on the arm with a stick*.—*adj.* (loosely) expert, as *a crack shot*.—*v.* to make a sharp sound, as *to crack your fingers together*: to partly split

Sometimes when you are looking up a word in a dictionary you will find that there are two or more words that seem to be exactly the same. To know which meaning you want you have to know which one of these words to look at.

One of the ways of telling one word from another is by thinking what it is doing in a sentence.

Some words in a sentence tell you the names of things or people. These are *nouns*. In a dictionary they will have the letter *n*. straight after them.

One or two words in a sentence tell you what is happening. These are *verbs*. In a dictionary a verb will have the letters *v*., *v.i.*, or *v.t.* after it.

Often there are some words in a sentence that tell you what something is like. These are called adjectives. In a dictionary they will have *adj.* after them.

Other words tell you how a thing is done, or tell you a bit more about the adjective. These are *adverbs*. They have *adv.* after them.

Head your work
8.3   Word match
Separating words that
look the same

You can separate these words by what 'part of speech' (n., v., adj., or adv.) they are. Look up the meanings for each and put each one down carefully.

1	frank	v.		9	post	n.[1]
2	frank	adj.		10	post	n.[2]
3	stamp	n.		11	post	v.
4	stamp	v.		12	post-	adv.
5	address	n.		13	seal	v.
6	address	v.		14	seal	n.[1]
7	public	adj.		15	seal	n.[2]
8	public	n.				

8.4 How to put it nicely

Head your work
8.4 Polite letters

Write one or two of these letters. Remember to lay out the envelopes each time. Choose the right phrases from the list above.

1   Write a polite letter to a mail order firm explaining why you cannot keep what they have sent, and asking for a replacement.

2   Write a letter asking a firm to send you a spare part for a machine you have bought from them.

3   Write a letter to a photographic processing firm asking why your colour prints are such a bad colour – is it your fault or theirs?

8.5 Newsy letters

You may find you need to write a newsy letter sooner than you expect. You may join the forces at 16 and be posted away from home; or get a temporary job in a hotel at the seaside; or just go away to explore.

The way you lay the letter out should be much the same as a business letter. The words you write can be much more chatty.

Look at this 'newsy' letter here.
1 Are Sally and David on holiday? How do you know?
2 Is David Sally's boyfriend? How do you know?
3 Which 'people' are quite decent?
4 What happened to Dave when he opened the washing-up machine?
5 Who is Sandy?

Seaside Hotel,
Sandcliffs,
Lancashire.

August 23rd,

Dear Mum and Dad,

We have been having a great time! Baking hot sunshine and lovely swimming! I'm as brown as a berry and Dave is quite sunburnt. Food is lovely and the people are quite decent.

Not too much to do really, so we get quite a while on the beach every day. Dave even goes fishing sometimes — he caught a big plaice the other day. Much bigger than the one he got years ago on the Isle of Man — remember?

You should have seen him in the kitchen the other day. There's a huge washing up machine that sprays hot water over everything for ages. Well you know how impatient he is. So of course he has to go and open it while it is working. He did look lovely with bits of bacon rind and wet breadcrumbs and tea leaves all over him! He needed a good scrub before he was ready to go on dinner waiting rota.

Lots of love,

Sally

P.S Give Sandy lots of pats and a big bone from me.

8.6 Write away!

Head your work
8.6 Write away!
(and the title if you
choose no 3. Otherwise
set it out as a letter.)

Choose one of the following, and write a piece over 200 words long about it.

1 **Write a newsy letter** to a friend or relation who is living some distance away. Can you make it a real one about things that are happening now — and really send it?

2 **Pretend you have gone on an expedition** to some distant place — mountains, or a desert island, or the Arctic or the Antarctic. Write the letter you would send home on the first mail after your arrival at the place you are exploring.

Sir Edmund Hilary and Tensing climbed Mount Everest in 1953.

3 **Stamp collecting.** If you are interested in stamps, write about the stamps you have got, how you look after and increase your collection, and what you would like to be able to get next. Are there any stamps you find particularly interesting or exciting?

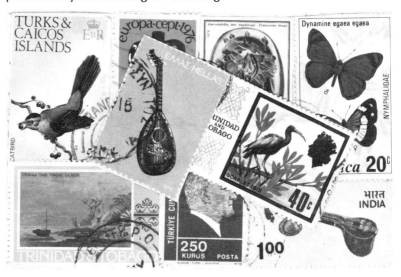

8.7   Controversy

Head your work
**8.7   Controversy about
letters and stamps**

1   I wouldn't want to use mail order catalogues anyway. It's like buying a pig in a poke.

2   It's not worth writing letters these days. You wait too long for an answer.
3   If you're too polite in a letter they'll not take any notice of you.
4   We shouldn't have the Queen's head on all our stamps, but we should put 'U.K.' instead.
5   British stamps are some of the best in the whole world.

8.8   Read all about it

When, in the War, the British Army needed to be brought back from the beaches at Dunkirk, the message went out that everyone who had a boat that could help should go to the rescue. It was a dangerous and difficult journey, and many strange boats were used for the crossing. One vivid story of the evacuation is *Snow Goose* by Paul Gallico. Although it is only quite a short book, it gives a very good impression of the dangers and the courage of the men involved.

Have you ever tried writing the story of a rescue? A rescue at sea, or in the mountains, or along a river? You might find it would be easier if you made it a newsy letter to a friend describing just what happened.

8.9 Crossword number eight

Clues across

1 We put letters into them before posting (9).

8 At the beginning of a race a runner puts this on the line (3).

9 A mother sheep (3).

*10 What the hot sun did to Dave's skin (5).

11 A short sleep (3).

13 Two letters that mean 'take special note of this', although in fact they stand for 'nota bene' (2).

14 A special sort of head-dress sometimes used by wealthy ladies (5).

16 Last two letters of the word 'words' (2).

17 Short for 'Lesley' (3).

18 The consonants in the word 'care' (2).

*19 A company that employs people (4).

21 Short way of saying thanks (2).

22 I ____ interested in stamps. Are you? (2).

*24 Be expecting something, like an answer to a letter (4).

*26 A special letter that says how well you have worked for someone (9).

Clues down

1 The letters after D S A in the alphabet (3).

* 2 Words that are often used for the subject of the sentence – they name things (5).

* 3 A word that tells us what is happening – it is about doing (5).

* 4 A written message (6).

5 A short cry of pain (2).

6 You may sometimes use this to write with (3).

* 7 To sort out one from another (8).

*12 The part around the North Pole where the sun never sets for at least one night of the year (6)

*15 It ____ expensive to send a letter (2).

*16 The first word of a letter (4).

*17 A lot of words arranged in a row (4).

20 The letters before N X F in the alphabet (3).

*23 'The one you sent ____ was the wrong size.' (2).

25 A word that describes things is ____ adjective (2).

9
Word families

9.1 How many letters are there in the alphabet?

Yes, you thought the answer was 26?
You were right.
But when you put *t* and *h* together the sound they stand for is quite different from the sound either stands for on its own.
The same is true of *s* and *h* (sh).
Or of *o* and another *o* (oo).
Or of *a*, followed by one consonant, and then by *e*.

In fact the words we say are made for far more than 26 separate sounds. As we have only 26 letter shapes to write these sounds down with, people have thought of the idea of putting 2 or 3 letters together to stand for a sound no single letter stands for.

How many 'letter groups' for different sounds can you find on the page opposite:
1   that have an *h* in them? (There are 5 of them.)
2   that have an *r* in them? (You should get 4.)
3   that have 2 vowels together in them? Take **y** as a vowel when it comes at the end of a word. (You should get 6.)
4   Could any of the 15 sounds you have written down to answer these three questions have been written with just one letter from the alphabet we have got? If so, which?

9.2   What comes next?

One of the ways of making it easier to learn English spelling is to get used to what letters *can* come next. There are, for example, *no* English words that end with just a *k* sound on its own except foreign names or words just arrived in the language (Kodak, anorak). Another safe rule is that the letter *q* is *always* followed with a *u* in true English words.

You can get used to what should come next in two ways:
1   By looking, noticing, and thinking about the spelling in each word as you read and write.
2   By joining up your letters when you write, so that an 'impossible' set of letters like iuqapz will not run easily off your pen.

Head your work
9.2   Spelling:
What comes next?

What letters would you expect to come next in these words:
1   any long word ending an _ _ like resistan _ _.
2   any fairly long word ending i _ _, like prepari _ _.
3   a long word ending at _ _ _, like associat _ _ _.
4   a word beginning s _ _, like s _ _ew. (There are several possible answers.)
5   a long word ending ib _ _, like incredib _ _.

Using your knowledge of what to expect next, can you fill in the missing letters in these words:
6   technic _ _ities
7   col _ ecti _ _
8   compla _ _ts
9   b _ ic _
10   relati _ _ _ s _ _ p
11   respo _ sibi _ _ _ y
12   unq _ esti _ _ _ ab _ _

9.3   Word match

Head your work
9.3   Word match
Meanings of five long words

You have just completed some long words. Five of them are noted below. What do they mean? Can you explain them in your own words? If not, use a dictionary to help you.

technicalities   association
responsibility   incredible
resistance

9.4 Some common spelling families

Spelling becomes easier to learn if you think of words in families.

Families, that is, that have a group of letters the same. The group of letters may well be one of those we were thinking of that stand for a sound that you cannot write down with one letter on its own.

The oa family

Head your work
9.4 Common spelling word families

A lot of short old homely words (words that the Saxons knew) have the letters -oa- in them.
Here are ten to start you off. Can you make the list up to 20?

road moat oak load coal groan throat hoarse coast oat

t b s g f m fl c r c

The dge family

This is another family of short words from the Saxons. Again they are homely, everday words. Many of them are words about things you can feel or touch.

Here are five to start you off. Can you make the list up to 10?

wedge ridge fledge badge splodge

e m h bu d

9.5 Families of another type

Many of our longer words have come from French and Latin.
They have different sorts of spellings.
They belong to different spelling families.
Many of these words are words about ideas — things you cannot see, touch, or feel.

Head your work
9.5 Spelling families for words about ideas

The -tion family
There are hundreds of long words that end in -tion.
Here are seven to start you off. How many more can you add? (Be careful with spelling the first parts.)

resignation
abolition
completion
motion

solution
attention
friction

The -ance/-ence family
There are lots of words ending with -ance or -ence. There is no easy way of knowing if the vowel near the end is an *a* or an *e*. You have to learn them bit by bit, or look them up.
What are these words?

-ance family nouns	-ence family nouns
what you look like: app__ance	letters sent: cor—ence
making difficulties: res—ance	knowing how to: com—ence
making a noise: dis—ance	keeping on at it: pers__ence
mattering a lot: imp__ance	doing very well: exc—ence
not knowing: ign—ance	blamelessness: inn—ence

**Head your work
9.6   Write away!
(and the title)**

9.6   Write away!

1   **My better way of spelling.** Changes I would like to see in spelling. Words that I would change. New letters I would invent. How I would organize the change.

2   **The world of the word families.** What sort of world is brought to mind by a word family? What things did the Saxons who made the **oa** and **dge** words know, like, and talk about? What things did the French, who made the **-tion** and **-ence** words, like? You could also think of the Saxon word family with **wh** and the French one that ends with **-ment** (government &c).

3   **What I know about other languages.** Do you know any other language yourself? Or know someone who does? French, German or Welsh perhaps, or someone who has come to England and used to speak Arabic, Punjabi, Swahili, Cantonese or some other language? What does it sound like? How is it spelt? What letters are different? What words do you know?

9.7   Controversy

1   American spelling is more sensible than ours.
2   It's time English spelling was reformed.
3   We shouldn't let new words keep coming in to the language.
4   Spelling ought to be controlled by:
a)   the government
b)   the teachers
c)   the newspapers
5   There's a right way of talking English, just as there is a right way of spelling it, and local dialects should be stamped out.

9.8   Read all about it

When someone writes a poem, he or she is usually trying to use the poetry to explain just how they feel about something they have experienced. Poetry is often a better way of saying it than the ordinary words of everyday speech. Even when there is no rhyme and no special pattern in the poem, the way the words are laid out, the sort of words that are chosen, and the sort of sentences that are used, make a sort of special occasion. This special occasion gives a chance to make one's own feelings quite plain.

When D. H. Lawrence saw a dangerous snake, he was not sure whether to kill it or to let it go. In a way he ought to kill it, just because it was dangerous. And yet it was also rather beautiful — until it slid away. Then when he saw it disappearing he found he did not like it so much. He tells us about his feelings for this snake in his poem 'Snake', which is one of many poems about animals that tell us how people feel about them.

Head your work
9.8 (with the one word
that says what you are
writing about)

Try to write a poem of your own to say how you feel about something. It might be an animal (cat? worm? slug?), or it might be a place or a vehicle (train? motorbike?). You do not need to use rhyme, but make sure that your words make a special occasion.

Clues across

1 A piece of paper can be _____ into bits (4).
3 Farmers keep these animals to give milk (4).
6 This insect looks a bit like a butterfly (4).
7 First half of the word 'cosmonauts' (5).
* 9 A Saxon one wound and twisted its way around the country (4).
10 A fruit rather like an apple, but longer (4).
*11 The Saxons used this sort of meal for porridge (3).
*12 One for everyone is one _____ (4).
*15 Short for 'is not' (4).
16 A short word people say to drive an animal away (4).
17 A large sort of wild cat that lives in America (4).
18 To aim wrongly (at a goal perhaps?) (4).
*21 Half of two (3).
22 Someone who comes from Libya (6).
23 Short for 'steam ship' (2).
24 A full container will have something _____ _____ (2, 2).
25 A person who comes from Denmark (4).
27 First three letters of 'Telstar' (3).
*28 Not over there (4).
29 The coloured part of your eye (4).
31 The one after this (4).
33 They make dreadful yowlings on the roofs at night (7).
*35 Another word for 'speak' (3).
*36 the opposite of 'no' (3).

9.9 Crossword number nine

Clues down

* 1 Special technical aspects of something (14).
* 2 Taking charge of something, and the blame if necessary (14).
* 3 Letters sent backwards and forwards (14).
4 Middle letters of the word 'motor' (3).
* 5 This sub-heading dealt with what you might expect to follow (4, 5, 4).
* 6 The Saxons would build one and fill it with water round each fortress (4).
8 Food from animals (4).
13 The letters before B I V O in the alphabet (4).
*14 When your throat hurts and it is not easy to talk (6).
18 A man who works underground digging coal (5).
19 The letters before T Z U in the alphabet (3).
20 Short for 'South Africa' (2).
26 Dialects are spoken in certain _____ or parts of the country (5).
30 English spelling is _____ difficult because the language has come from _____ many different peoples (2).
32 Last two letters of the word 'floats' (2).
34 It belongs to me. It is _____ pen (2).

10
Public meetings

A — There are a lot of kids around that never go to ordinary schools, Comprehensives and the like. They go to these expensive 'public schools'. I don't think they should be allowed to.

B — Why not? Their parents pay for them, don't they? They pay more than £1,000 a year to send them there. If they want to pay more than £5 for every day at school, why shouldn't they?

A — But the kids become snobs, don't they? They think they're better than the rest of us because their parents can pay all that.

B — Aren't they snobs before they go to the public schools? Most of them live in big posh houses.

A — Well, how would they get on if they came here? What would you do to them? They'd have to mix with us, wouldn't they? Do 'em good to see how the rest of us live and think. When they leave school they get all the big jobs and start pushing us around. They're all the same, the bosses in the factories and the ones in the Corporation.

B — It's a matter of brains, not your school, whether you're boss or not.

A – Rot! What brains has that fool in the Housing Department got? Yet he tells us all we can't even paint the outside of our houses, because they belong to the stupid Corporation! If he'd gone to school with ordinary kids, kids who live in Council houses and flats, he'd see. Pig-headed he is. Brought up by a nanny in a big posh house, do what you like there, so long as you don't mix with the kids down the road. Oh no, don't speak to them, Johnny nose in air.

B – But I can't see why you should stop them. It's a free country. If you want a posh car you pay for it and buy it. If you want a posh house you save up and get it. You don't have to live in a Council house. Why should you *have* to go to a state school? *Your* parents spend a lot of their money in the pub, and on the pools, and going round in your super car. If someone else wants to spend his money on a school for his kids, why shouldn't he?

A – Look 'ere, mate. If my dad gets done for speeding, and one of them posh blokes gets done for doing the same speed, would you like it if the posh bloke is allowed to slip the copper a fiver and get away with it? But you know and he knows that if he tries that one, he'll end up in clink. Why should his kid get sent to a different school just because he's got cash to throw around?

B – By the way, you're forgetting something. Half the kids in these 'public schools' live there, because their parents are on jobs away from home. Where can they go if you close all the boarding schools?

A – Now that just shows how little you know. Didn't you know the state has boarding schools too, for ordinary kids? Not kids that have to go there, but just ones that want to go to a boarding school.

Head your work
10.1 Arguing about private schools

1   How many people are discussing public schools?
2   Have they finished their discussion? Can you think of anything else they might discuss? (Taxes? How old some pupils are? What they learn?)
3   What does the first speaker think should happen to public schools?
4   Give three different reasons why the second speaker thinks that public schools should be allowed to go on.
5   Has either speaker been a pupil in a public school? Is there any proof in what they say?

10.2   Having an argument

Some people shout.
Some people fight.
Some people slam the door behind them.
Some people howl.
And some people can keep their end up.

Look back at the piece 'Down with the Public Schools!'.
1   What words were used to show that the speakers were getting cross?
2   Were there any times when one speaker was rude to the other? If so, what was said that was rude?
3   Did each speaker listen to the other speaker and answer what the other one had said? The first speaker has six turns and the second has five turns. Which of these, if any, did not answer what the speaker before said?
4   How often did one speaker interrupt another?
5   Are the speakers seeing new points from the other side that they hadn't thought of before? Which points were they?

10.3   Word match

Head your work
10.3   Word match
Names of schools

There are many different types of school in Britain. Make a list of the ones mentioned here, saying which pupils each school is for. How many of these types have you ever been in to? (For example, when playing a match.)

Infant, Junior, Primary, Preparatory, Middle, Junior High, Senior High, Comprehensive, Public, Grammar, Secondary Modern, Technical College.

Free, over 16, full time or part time.
State school (free), age 5–7.
State school (free), for those who pass the exam to get in, age 11–16 (or 18 if you like).
State school (free), ages 7–11.
State school (free), age 5–11.
Private school (you pay), age 7–13.
State school (free), age 11–16, but you probably don't go if you pass the exam when you are 11.
Private school (you pay), age 14–16 (or 18 if you like).
State school (free) usually age 10–12.
State school (free) usually age 11–13.
State school (free) usually age 14–16 (or 18 if you like).
State school (free) age 11–16 (or 18 if you like).

A secondary boarding school run by Essex County Council.

10.4 Mind benders

Does the crowd matter?
The banners and the shouting?
The show of hands in a vote?
Would you put your hand up for 'no' in a meeting where they had voted 'yes' like this?
Would you begin to think the speakers must be right when so many people vote 'yes'?

Sometimes at meetings the crowds stop the speaker being heard.
They start a chant.
They throw eggs and tomatoes.
They shout questions all the time.

Head your work
10.4   Public meetings

1   Do you think the people who shout at meetings want to hear the other side of the argument? If not, why not?
2   Do you think they may be afraid of the other side of the argument? Why could anyone be *afraid* of it?
3   If you are listening to an argument, would you like to hear both sides?
4   How do you like to make up your mind about something?
a) by hearing what your leader thinks?
b) by thinking about all the points that anyone can bring up?
5   Would you trust a leader who shouts down the other side?

10.5 The power of words

**Head your work
10.5 The power of
words**

Words can change our lives.
1 What single sentence do most lovers hope will make all the difference to their lives?
2 What one or two words make an enormous difference to someone standing in dock at the end of a court case?
3 What do you hope to hear when you apply for a job?
In many countries the Government tries to control the power of words.
- You are not allowed to hear anything you like.
- You are not allowed to say anything you like.
- You are not allowed to read anything you like.
4 Why do you think many Governments want to limit the power of words? What might happen if words were free there?
5 What sort of words would a Government want to stop people using?
There are very few countries that are as free as Britain.
Here is a list of things that are crimes in some countries.
You could be shot, tortured, imprisoned or exiled for doing them. Which of these things are not allowed in the United Kingdom?
6 To believe in God.
7 To belong to any religious group.
8 To suggest we stop having H.R.H. the Queen (or King).
9 To say the Government is rotten and must go.
10 To go abroad when you want to.
11 To write or telephone to anyone you like in the world.
12 To make a speech or call a meeting.

Dr Sakharov, the Nobel peace-prize winner, travelled more than 5,000 miles from Moscow into the wilderness of Siberia last month, seeking out a friend who had been exiled there.

His friend, who is 36, was secretary of the small Soviet branch of Amnesty International, the London-based organization concerned with political prisoners. He was sentenced last April to five years' exile, for anti-Soviet slander, and sent to Yakutskaya, one of the country's most remote regions, as a labourer in a saw-mill.

Determined to see how he was faring, the Sakharovs flew to Mirnyy. From there, they had to catch a small aircraft that flew, when weather permitted, to a dirt airstrip at Nyurba, a smaller town about 160 miles to the east. They were told that no tickets to Nyurba were available.

After waiting for about 27 hours, they caught their flight to Nyurba. More than 12 miles were left to the hamlet in which their friend was exiled.

Rebuffed when they asked for a car ride, the Sakharovs set out on foot down the unpaved road. A captain of the Soviet highway police came up to warn them that they would get lost in the forest. After they had walked two miles the captain, who knew who they were, drove up and offered them a lift.

When they got in, Mrs Sakharov said, he turned the car around and drove them back to where they had started. Though it was growing dark, the Sakharovs started walking again. A passing driver stopped to apologize that police had told him not to pick them up.

They arrived at the village about 3 a.m. Since it was Sunday, they planned to spend the day together, but their friend's superior appeared to tell him that he would have to go to work as an unpaid workday for the state.

Two geologists had arrived earlier, saying they were looking for mineral water in the frozen soil, and settled in just the other side of the wall, Mrs Sakharov said. She identified them as secret police agents.

1   What is a Nobel Peace Prize and how does someone win it?

2   What is a political prisoner?

3   What does Amnesty International do?

4   What is slander?

5   Name a place 5,000 miles away from where you live. How much does it cost to get there?

10.6   Write away!

**Head your work
10.6   Write away!
(and the title)**

1   **They don't know what they're missing.** Imagine someone in a school quite different from yours. What could you say about your school and your free-time activities that would make them think they were missing something?

2   **The world of the permit.** Imagine that you live in one of the less free countries. Tell the story of your life when you need to have a permit to move house, to change job, to travel; when the only candidates in an election all belong to the same party, and you have got to vote; where the only radio is the Government one, and the only books are in Government shops.

3   **What I would like to stop.** If you were a dictator, what controls and regulations would you want to make? What do you see going on around you that you would like to stop? What do the others in your class think of your proposals?

10.7   Controversy

**Head your work
10.7   Controversy
about freedom**

1   Is it good policy to allow some pupils to be sent to public schools?
2   Should everyone have exactly the same education, or should they have the same *chances* for education? (What is the difference here?)
3   We allow too much freedom in our country. It's asking for trouble to allow people to join the political parties that want to limit the freedom of some of our people.
4   Printing workers should never go on strike because they don't like what they are asked to put in print.
5   We've fought for our freedom in wars, and now we don't value what we've got.

10.8   Read all about it

Many people have never come into contact with real religious feeling. You can't call most school Assemblies, or the R.E. lessons, religious at all.
The story of how some New York toughs came into contact with religion is told in *The Cross and the Switchblade*, by David Wilkerson. It's an exciting book, and easy to read.
If you see how strong the power of words was for these gangsters, you can begin to see why Communist governments are so frightened of allowing any religion in their countries.
Can you write an account of the most moving experience of your life? What it was, how it happened, and how you felt?

**Head your work
10.8   A very special
thing happened**

10.9 Crossword number ten

Clues across

* 1 Schools you have to pay to go to (6, 7).
9 Short for 'Ordnance Survey' (2).
*10 The sort of school that older pupils (over 14) go to (6).
11 Last two letters of the word 'battle' (2).
*12 A word for supposing (2).
13 First two letters of the word 'dwell' (2).
14 Short for 'Alfred' (3).
*17 People who are said to walk with their noses in the air (5).
20 Not now, but some time after (5).
*22 A school for all the pupils aged from 11 to 16 or 18 (13).
*26 Belonging to you (4).
*27 Short for 'Her Royal Highness' (3).
28 The bend in your leg (4).
29 The letters after Y F H in the alphabet (3).
30 Vowels in the word 'limit' (2).

31 To use power – or something heavy, like a mallet (5).
*33 Short word used instead of a man's name (2).
*34 A lady who looks after small children (5).
37 Consonants in the word 'noun' (2).
*38 Our country – England, Scotland, Wales, Northern Ireland, the Isle of Man, the Channel Islands, and the Orkney and Shetland Islands (6, 7).

Clues down

* 1 A plan or idea (6).
* 2 Make use of (3).
* 3 You were asked to say which pupils each school ___ ___ (2, 3).
4 Last two letters of 'police' (2).
5 Consonants in the word 'seen' (2).
6 Short for 'Criminal Investigation Department' (3).

* 7 A loud cry (4).
* 8 Either this __ that (2).
*12 Things that have been printed (2, 5).
*14 School assemblies are not religious __ all (2).
15 Flat or even (5).
*16 Being able to do what you want to (7).
17 Being pleased with yourself (4).
*18 You might slam the door _____ you (6).
19 To get smaller (6).
*21 Saying something in a question (6).
23 Liquid does this when it comes out slowly (4).
24 A noise that asks a question (2).
*25 Not out (2).
*32 Can you keep yours up in an argument? (3).
33 A grunt of disgust (2).
35 Vowels in the word 'change' (2).
36 The letters after X H in the alphabet (2).

11
What about a job?

11.1 The donkey bit

Foreman:	Hello lad. What can we do for you?
Boy:	I'm John Barnes. I was told to start work here this morning.
Foreman:	Ah! That's right! Well, you came just the right moment, lad. I've been looking all over for my donkey bit and I can't find it anywhere. Pop along to Ted in the Drawing Office and ask him if he's got it.
Ted:	His donkey bit? No, not seen it for ages. Let me give you a tip. Go and ask old Steve in the Pattern Shop. He ought to have it.
Steve:	No, not me. Try Fred on the Assembly line. It's the sort of thing he might want.
Fred:	So you're a new lad here are you? Got a lot to learn yet, me lad. John your name is? No, John, I've not got his donkey bit and I've not had it for a long while since. You'd better get along quick to the Paint Shop. The boss'll be mad with you being so long getting it. By the way, lad, did you ever know . . .
Alf in paint shop:	Donkey bit? No good looking here. We never use it. Try the loading bay. Ask Greg.
Greg:	No, I've not got it today. You could ask Sue in the canteen though. Better be quick before they get busy with lunch.

Sue:	What does he think I'd want that for? The Secretaries in the typing pool might have it though. Ask Sheila.
Sheila.	No, not me. You could ask Sharon, the P.R.O.
Sharon:	Never seen it! I don't even know what it looks like. Never heard of it except a few times when new lads come round asking for it. I always send them to Betty in the computer room.
Betty:	No, the computer doesn't need it. Ask the MD's secretary, Mrs Roberts. Knock and wait for an answer before you go in.
Mrs Roberts:	Now you go back to the Foreman and tell him you've looked all over the works and you can't find it anywhere. Be quick or it'll be lunch time.
Foreman:	Everywhere? Even the loading bay? And the canteen? Ah well, I'll have to make do without it. Good lad, now you know your way round the works and you've met the people in charge of each part. Now what I want you to begin on is . . .

**Head your work
11.1   Looking for
a donkey bit**

1   What sort of place is John starting work at?
2   How long did he spend looking for the donkey bit? Why did it take so long?
3   How many places did he visit looking for it?
4   Do you think there really was a donkey bit to look for?
5   What clues did John get as he went round that he was on a wild goose chase?

11.2   What's about?

Have you started looking for a job yet?
Each workplace has different sorts of jobs to offer:
as receptionists, apprentices, trainees, clerks, secretaries
and typists.
In the workplace they know what all these jobs are called.
They use the words every day. They may be surprised if
you are not sure about all of them.

**Head your work
11.2   What jobs are
about?**

1   What are the biggest places of employment in your area?
2   Which ones of the smaller places of employment in your district often have jobs suitable for 16-year-olds? What jobs are there?
3   How many small and unusual jobs can you name that are done in your district?
4   What ideas have you got so far about what you would like to do when you leave school?
5   Do you know if you are likely to have the right exams to get the job you are thinking about?

Head your work
11.3   Word match:
Words about jobs

11.3   Word match

Set out a clear table showing these names, their abbreviations if they have any, and what they really mean. (One is done for you.)

C.S.E.   C. & G.   O.N.C.   H.N.C.   O-level   A-level
C.E.E.   day release,   block release,   residential course,
probationary period,   apprentice,   degree,   graduate,
trainee.

Name of qualification or course	What it means	Details about it
C.S.E.	Certificate of Secondary Education	Exam done in school at age 16.

Words to help you

advanced	certificate	city	education
extended	guilds	higher	national
ordinary	secondary		

Details
Exam done in school at age 16.
Exam done at college from 16+.
Exam done in school, usually at 17.
Exam done in college from 16+ (difficult).
Exam done in school, usually at 18.
Exam done in college from 18+ (very difficult).
Exam done at university from 21+ (very difficult).
Person who has done a degree at a university.
When a person is working for a trial period.
Training course where a person sleeps away from home.
When a person has one day a week at college as part of the paid work.
When a person has a few weeks at a time at college as part of the paid work.
Person on a four-year full-time training course that will qualify him as a skilled worker.
Person on a training course arranged by the firm, with no fixed length and no fixed qualification at the end.

11.4 Skilled or unskilled?

The tale of Jean McQueen

There was a girl called Jean McQueen,
Who longed for when she was sixteen.
One thought she kept within her head,
She thought all day, she thought in bed,
That nothing better could there be,
But to work in a factory.
To sit and stitch and chat all day
And then to take home all that pay!
No work in school was ever done
While she sat longing for the fun.
A month of work beside the bench,
And getting her cards was not a wrench
When her Department got the chop —
Much more fun to serve in a shop.
She weighed and wrapped and smiled until
She thought she did it all with skill.
One day a friend said 'Jean McQueen,
Why don't you work in our canteen?'
She scraped and mashed and served the food,
Until her tiff when she was rude
And the Supervisor was angry — very!
Next a job as a Secretary,
Filing and typing and making tea,
But she and the keyboard could never agree.
An interesting job as a receptionist
Was the next occupation on her list.
Ringing and lifting and talking all day,
But always the same dull thing to say.
She couldn't think of anything worse,
So next she'd train to be a nurse.
Just then along came Jim McKing,
Who tucked her nicely under his wing:
'You've done enough, Jean, in your life,
Now you're just ready to come as my wife.'

**Head your work
11.4   Skilled or
unskilled?**

1   What good reasons are there for not worrying too
much if you don't stay in your first job?
2   What good reasons are there for finding a good job and
sticking to it?
3   What jobs become more difficult to get as you get
older? What age limits are there for apprenticeships,
nursing, police cadets, or firemen?
4   Is it better to have a temporary job than no job at all?
5   Is it better to stay at school rather than go on the dole?

11.5　Picking up ideas

What can you find out about work from people you know?

Between you, in the class, there must be a lot of brothers and sisters, boy friends and girl friends, neighbours and old school friends, who have jobs.

**Head your work
11.5　Do they like their work?**

Try to collect some information about what they are all doing, and how much they like their work. Don't ask about the pay. You might get wrong answers. You might like to set out your class results like this:

Name	Age	Left school in	Exams passed	Now working for	Job now is, or unemployed	Training	Jobs held before	Nicest thing about work is

11.6　Write away!

**Head your work
11.6　Write away!
(and the title)**

**Head your work
11.7　Controversy about jobs**

1　**The job I'd love to have,** and what I would like about it. Choose something that you **could** really do — you can't be King or Queen of Britain! Why would you like it? What do you think is the best part of it? Would it be nice all the time?

2　**The tale of Jim McKing.** The Tale of Jean McQueen is a rough sort of rhyming called 'doggerel'. Can you make a doggerel rhyme about Jim McKing or anyone else?

3　**Doing a difficult job.** Is there something you can do that needs quite a bit of explaining? Something you excel at? Making a dress? Catching fish? Stripping an engine? Enlarging a photograph? Explain carefully how to do it so that someone who doesn't know how can do it too.

11.7　Controversy

1　Schools make too much fuss about what job you're going to get. You should just see what turns up.
2　Teenagers are paid too much compared with what they get later on, and they get used to having too much pocket money.
3　No Government should allow 16-year olds to be unemployed. They could avoid it if they . . .
4　It's unfair to use exam results to choose people for jobs.
5　Everyone is equal, so everyone should be paid the same. Why should a miner get more than a farm worker?

11.8   Read all about it!

Have you read *Tom Sawyer* or *Huckleberry Finn* by Mark Twain? If so, you probably never realized that the man who wrote the story piloted big boats for a living.

The boats he piloted were the big paddle steamers, and his journeys were up and down the Mississippi River. The journeys were over a thousand miles long – as far as from England to the Mediterranean – and the river is so wide in parts that you can hardly see the banks. Yet it is full of mudbanks to catch any ship that goes in the wrong bit.

It was a difficult job to learn, and he tells about it in the *Life on the Mississippi*.

Head your work
11.8   A worker's tale

Have you ever done a job (paper job, Saturday job)?
Or helped out someone (digging a garden, baby minding)?
Have you any tales to tell of people with unusual characters that you have worked for?

11.9 Crossword number eleven

Clues across

* 1   Not having a job to go to (10).
*10   A young lady (4).
 11   First half of the word 'vote' (2).
 12   Short for 'road' (2).
*13   Not any (government, for example) (2).
*14   Short for 'Gregory' (4).
 16   To do something without difficulty is to do it with _____ (4).
 19   To suspend, or put a picture on the wall (4).
*20   Someone who is being trained for a skilled job (10).
 24   The word for a hen producing an egg (3).
 25   First half of the word 'rich' (2).
 26   When you have no choice – neither this _____ that (3).
*27   Not out (2).
 28   A competition to see who can get to the finishing post first (4).

*30   Ted said, 'Let _____ give you a tip' (2).
*31   John was told _____ start work (2).
*32   To be particularly good at something (5).
*34   The way out of a building (4).
 36   The letters before T B T J in the alphabet (4).
*37   A section or division of a factory or school (10).

Clues down

 2   You _____ your head to agree (3).
* 3   Two letters that mean 'for example', although they stand for the Latin words *exempli gratia* (2).
* 4   Someone who works underground (5).
* 5   Short for 'Public Relations Officer' (3).
 6   Last two letters of the word 'skill' (2).

* 7   Should do (5).
 8   One, three and five are 'odd' numbers. Two, four and six are _____ numbers (4).
* 9   A rough sort of verse with rhyme (8).
*12   Thought of, woken up to (8).
 15   Water that comes from the sky (4).
 17   A cook fries fish in _ _____ (1, 3).
 18   His job is to find out secrets (3).
 21   A long period of years (3).
*22   The one you like best (6).
 23   What your boss might call out when you knock on his door (4,2).
 28   An order that you take turns in (4).
*31   A hint or a word of advice (3).
*33   An examination taken at 16 by a large number of school pupils (3).
 35   The last two letters of the word 'axe' (2).

12
Newspapers

12.1 Words, words, words

'And now the news, read by Colin Peters.'
What follows?
Fifteen minutes of reading and film?
How much has he read?

Head your work
12.1 Hearing
the news

1 If the broadcast news was printed in a newspaper, do you think it would fill:
a) a whole newspaper
b) four sides
c) one side
d) less than a side.
(In fact there is far more printed in a big newspaper than could be read in a whole day of television news features!)
2 How many main news stories has he read about?
3 Were you able to pick and choose what you heard about and how much you heard about it?
4 What advantages have newspapers got compared with television or radio?
5 Were you able to see a lot of pictures of the news and hear it very soon after it happened?
6 What advantages has television (or radio) got compared with newspapers?

12.2　Got a paper job?

Everyone who has had a paper job ought to find the next questions easy to answer!

1　What national daily papers are there?
2　Which of these are the 'popular' papers (with the smaller pages)?
3　Which of these are the 'quality' papers (with the bigger pages)?

A national daily newspaper is one that is printed in one or two places and taken all over the country. In every town you could go to today you could buy a copy of that paper that would be almost the same as yours. The only difference would be that some copies would be 'early' editions and some would be 'late' ones.

Most of the national daily papers sell well over a million copies a day. All these are printed during the night, early enough to be in the paper shops by six in the morning.

Printing at a newspaper press.

4　Have you ever thought what this printing involves? If the papers are printed for 10 hours during the night, and 1,200,000 copies are sold, how many copies are printed in one hour?
5　And how many copies are printed in one minute?
6　What is the circulation of the best selling paper of all just now – and how many copies a minute are printed of that paper?

As well as the national papers there are:
● local daily papers in almost every city
● national weekly papers, mostly on Friday, Saturday or Sunday
● local weekly papers
● national magazines, weekly or monthly

7　What local papers are there in your area?
8　What national weekly papers have you seen?
9　What national magazines have you seen?
10　Try to arrange a class exhibition of national magazines and then make notes about them. If you all bring in ones from home (model railway, women's magazines, sport and pop music papers etc.), you should be able to make a big display.

12.3　Word match

Can you explain what these words mean? Use a dictionary to help you on any you don't know.

1　journalist
2　editor
3　reporter
4　wholesaler
5　magazine
6　journal
7　newsagent
8　publish

USELESS EUSTACE

"Look—if I tell you the greyhound results do you promise to go away and leave me in peace?"

12.4   What's in a paper?

How much of the paper do you read?
Headlines?
Sport?
The Stars?
Your favourite cartoon?
What else is there in a national daily newspaper?

Look for these things:
1   News items — things that have just happened.
2   Comment — what the people who write the paper think about what has happened or what the government has done.
3   Features — special reports that could have been put in on another day without being out of date — who the new star is, all the transfers in a team during the year.
4   Sport report — news just about different sorts of sport (which sports?).
5   Cartoons — whether a daily 'strip' cartoon or the sort that is really a comment on some of the news.
6   Advertisements — none of the adverts are written by the newspaper people. They are made by the people who pay to have them put it.
7   Photographs, to cover the news.
8   Photographs, in features, pin-ups etc.

**Head your work
12.4   The national daily papers**

Make a table of all the national dailies and get a recent copy of each of them.
Put down *how many* of each of the 8 things in this list you can find in each newspaper. What differences are there between the papers?

Name of paper	News	Comment	Features	Sport	Cartoon	Adverts	Photos — news	Photos — features

12.5   Bias

When you are writing a report it is easy to let your own feelings show up. Sometimes this is done on purpose.

When these feelings are that a player played badly (or well), or the Government has done right (or wrong), it is called *bias*. Other people would have a *bias* the other way.

**Head your work
12.5   The kindest bias**

In each of the examples opposite, choose the one that is most biased *in favour* of the people concerned.

1 a) John Best fouls again.
  b) John Best scores 2 goals.
  c) John Best saves the day.
2 a) £ millions cut off V.A.T.
  b) Dennis the Menace strikes again.
  c) Income tax up, V.A.T. down.
3 a) Weather men wrong twice a week.
  b) More than half weather forecasts accurate.
  c) Odds 5:2 on for clever forecasters.
4 a) Neighbour's house a 'pigsty'.
  b) Neighbour kept pets in garden.
  c) Complaint against neighbour dismissed as 'rubbish'.
5 a) Jane West swims to victory.
  b) Jubilant Jane the superb swimmer.
  c) Slow time but Jane scrapes home first.

Head your work
12.6   Write away!
(and the title)

12.6   Write away!

1   **My favourite paper** (or magazine). Which one do you like best, and which bits of it do you read most? Would other people find the same bits best? Why would you recommend them?

2   **Why I always go out when the news comes on,** or **Why I never read the papers I deliver.**

3   Write a **News Report**, or a **Feature** for your local paper — either about school or home interests. Give it a good headline, and set it out to interest other people. Where and when did the event happen?

Pupils at local school raise money in charity walk

12.7 Controversy

**Head your work
12.7 Controversy
about the news**

1 The news spends too much time on violence. There ought to be more about . . .

2 Newspapers are too fat. It's a waste of paper.

3 There's too much news from abroad. Enough happens in Britain to fill every news bulletin or newspaper.

4 British people never take enough interest in the rest of the world.

5 The most important thing that happened yesterday was . . .

12.8 Read all about it

A scene from *Murder on the Orient Express*.

Have you ever tried reading a detective story? You have probably seen hundreds of detective films on television. How good are you at working out who is the crook? One famous author of detective stories is Agatha Christie. You might like to look at one of her books in the library? They will probably have a lot of her books on one shelf there. Another famous author is Arthur Conan Doyle. See if you can write a short detective story of your own. Would your detective be Sherlock Holmes — or yourself? You would be wise to think out what the clues would be before you begin writing, so that you can bring them in carefully at the right time.

12.9 Crossword number twelve

Clues across

* 1 Pictures that come into your home from far away (10).
  8 Something to put over your head (4).
  9 A short word meaning 'you and me' (2).
*10 A big town (4).
*13 Different, fresh, not old (3).
*14 Rain, sun, wind or snow (7).
*16 The short word for 'advertisements' (3).
  17 Some papers make a profit and some make a ＿＿ (4).
  19 First half of the word 'sink' (2).
  20 A deep channel along a road (3).
  21 The sort of money they have in Italy (4).
*23 Short for 'it is' (3).
  25 Short for 'physical education' (2).
  26 You wash with it (4).
  27 A distinction between one thing and another (10).
  29 Short for 'executive officer' (2).
  30 Last three letters of the word 'shepherd' (3).
  31 First three letters of the word 'aeroplane' (3).

  32 Snow collected up for throwing (8).
  35 You read the newspaper, but you ＿＿ pictures on a screen (3).
  36 It is for you. It is ＿＿ newspaper (4).

Clues down

  1 When the frost and snow melts (4).
  2 Vowels in the word 'hello' (2).
* 3 The sort of paper that is only sold in one area (5).
* 4 The person who puts the reports in a newspaper together (6).
  5 First half of the word 'sold' (2).
  6 Jane paid Bob the money she ＿＿ him (4).

* 7 Where you can read the news (10).
  11 Last two letters of the word 'growth' (2).
*12 Newspapers tell you particularly about this day (9).
*13 For the whole country (8).
*15 Batches of newspapers printed at one particular time (8).
*18 Extremely good (6).
*19 Sheets or pages (5).
  21 The letters before M T F in the alphabet (3).
*22 A competition to see who gets there first (4).
  24 Short for 'Science Fiction' (2).
  28 Not many (3).
  33 Vowels in the word 'poem' (2).
  34 First half of the word 'look' (2).

13
Types of books

13.1   The library? Ugh! What a sight!

'Go in there? Catch me!'

'What's wrong with it?'

'All those books!'

'Some of them are good.'

'Catch *me* reading a book! Everyone would laugh.'

'More fool them. Most people love books – at any rate some kinds.'

'What do you like, then?'

'A good ghost story to make your hair stand on end, or a war story with lots of fighting. Or an escape. Something quick and racey.'

'But it's horrible in there!'

'It's just a big room. Why is it different from any other room?'

'You have to be so quiet.'

'Not as quiet as all that. You can talk softly you know.'

'Why can't you talk as loud as you like?'

'Well, when I'm choosing a book I often read two or three pages to see if I like it. Then I like to think about the book. I don't want to keep hearing what they're saying at the other side of the room.'

'But they fine you if you keep the book long.'

'Stupid word! Why those daft librarians ever called it a fine *I* don't know. You'd not mind paying a few pence to hire a bike, or a boat, for a bit, would you? I can't see why the librarians don't just say you can have the book free for two or three weeks, and then there's a hire charge of a penny a day or whatever. You'd not mind then would you?'

'Spose not. But then I could never find a decent book in all that lot.'

'Come on in and I'll show you. I always go straight to the shelves marked 'war', or the ones marked 'ghost stories'. Where would you like to begin?'

Head your work
13.1   Libraries

1   How many libraries have you ever been in?

2   Do you often borrow books from a library?

3   Which local libraries are you allowed to borrow books from if you want to?

4   Which local libraries do you know your way around?

5   Do the libraries make a charge if you keep the book long? How long, and how much?

6   How many books can readers have out at a time from each library?

7   Can you renew books when you want to?

8   What sections are labelled in your local libraries?

13.2   Putting books in order

There's no point having lots of books if you can't quickly find the one you want.

All librarians think of two main sorts of books – **fiction** (made up stories) and **non-fiction** (true books). They put each sort in a separate part of the library.

Head your work
13.2   Finding the book you want

1   What sort of book is this one you are using? Fiction or non-fiction?
If it is a fiction book, the librarian looks to see who wrote it (the author) or who collected the stories together (the editor). She then puts it with any other books by the same author or editor.
Sometimes the fiction section is broken into different types of story – war stories, crime stories and so on.
Authors are arranged in alphabetical order. Sometimes the first three letters of their surname are written in big letters on the back of the books.
So if you like one book someone wrote, it should be very easy to find some more books by the same person.
And if you know who wrote a story you are looking for, just look through the alphabetical order until you find his (or her) books.

2   Which of these books would you find nearest the 'beginning' of the shelving in a library: *The Dambusters* by P. Brickhill, *Tramps in Armour* by H. Forbes, *All Quiet on the Western Front* by E. M. Remarque?
If it is a non-fiction book, the librarian looks to see what it is about. She then puts it on a shelf with other books on the same subject. If you want a book about trains, you should find it among several other books about trains, so you can choose which you like best.
Non-fiction books usually have three numbers written on the back of the book. Sometimes these numbers have a decimal point and more numbers after it.

Index cards

If you have no idea where to look for books about trains, you can look up 'Trains' in the non-fiction card index in the library. This will give you the three numbers that are on the train books, and you can look through the shelves for them. If you have no idea who wrote a story but you do know what it is called, you can look up the title in the 'Fiction Index — Titles' and that will tell you the name of the author. Make sure you can use a library — the school one or a local one.

3   What three numbers are on the back of books about these things?
a) motorbikes
b) horses
c) sport
d) gardening

4   Who wrote these books?
a) Jane Eyre
b) Animal Farm
c) Lady Chatterley's Lover
d) Gulliver's Travels

5   How many books are there on the shelves just now about these topics, and what are the books called?
a) fashion
b) pop music
c) fishing
d) tennis

6   How many books are there on the shelves just now by
a) Agatha Christie
b) Conan Doyle
c) Ian Fleming
d) Ernest Hemingway.

13.3   Word match

Here is a list of different types of books. Explain what you would expect to find in the books of each type. Use a dictionary to help you if you need it. (One is done for you.)

Head your work
13.3   Word match
Types of books

Romance
War
Crime
Anthologies — collections of poems or short stories usually by different people.
Novels
Classics
Biographies
Autobiographies
Folk tales

13.4 What sort of reading have you looked at?

Head your work
**13.4   Types of reading
I have tried**

Make a list of all the types of reading that you have ever sampled. You might like to begin by putting down all the books and stories you can remember reading. Or you might like to sort out a selection of books in the classroom. You might find this list helpful while working on your own list:

folk tales	verse	travel	children's books
biography	exploration	drama	sport
novels	historical	war	non-fiction
religious	romance	classics	autobiography
ghost stories			

13.5   Bookshops

Head your work
13.5   Buying books

Have you ever bought any books? If you have, how many books have you ever bought?

Have you bought them from:
newsagents?   bookstalls?   stationers?   bookshops?

An illustration from *Martin Chuzzlewit* by Charles Dickens

1　Newsagents and bookstalls do not usually have a very big range of books. Which of the types of books on the list below would probably be hard to find in a newsagent or a bookstall, but could be found in a bookshop?

a) love stories
b) thrillers
c) books about stamp collecting
d) books about cooking
e) books about mechanics
f) books about yachting
g) books by Charles Dickens
h) books by C. S. Forester (the *Hornblower* books)?

2　Where can you buy books within ten miles of your home? Roughly how many books has each shop got, and what sorts of books are they? Are there any secondhand bookshops? Try to visit as many of the bookshops as possible.

3　How are the books arranged in the bookshops?
by series
by author
by price
by subject
by size

4　Do you know anyone who belongs to a book club? What books can they get cheaply that way? How much do they save?

13.6　Write away!

**Head your work
13.6　Write away!
(and the title)**

1　**A super book.** Choose any book you like (fiction or non-fiction) and say what you like about it – the story, the information it gives, the illustrations, the way it is printed and laid out, the way it has been written.

2　**My own story.** What sort of story do you like: Romance, Crime, Detective, any other? Have a go at writing a short story of your own of one of these types. You might like to think of your favourite story to help you begin.

3　**£1,000 Library.** If you had £1,000 to spend to set up a library for yourself and your friends, what sort of books would you buy, and how many books of each type would you try to get? Be careful to check the prices of some new books to get an idea how cheap the cheapest are, and what sorts of books are the most expensive.

Riddle
Why did the Librarian marry the policeman?

Because he was so good at booking.

13.7   Controversy

1   All librarians seem to be fierce old spinsters, who don't really want you to borrow books.
2   There aren't nearly enough local libraries run by the Council.
3   They don't buy the right books in the library. There ought to be more books about . . .
4   I will never buy a book. If I want one I'll borrow it from the library.
5   Books are important but too expensive. The Government ought to put a subsidy on the price.

13.8   Read all about it!

Do you like ghost stories? There are thousands of stories to choose from: most libraries have shelves specially for them.

Have you ever tried writing a ghost story yourself? Have a go and see what you can do.

13.9   Crossword number thirteen

Clues across

* 1   Collections of stories, usually by different people (11).

*11   A book written about someone's life (9).

13   Letters after S B in the alphabet (2).

*15   The girl asked 'What _____ you like then?' (2).

17   Letters after A Y in the alphabet (2).

*18   Not all, but more than a few (4).

19   The first half of 'half'! (2).

*20   Author of the *Hornblower* books (8).

*23   Last three letters of 'Thorp' (3).

*25   The way you can talk in a library (6).

*28   People who are using the books in a library (7).

*32   Not any (idea) (2).

*33   It should _____ easy to find a book (2).

*34   Books that have stories in them (7).

35   It shines in the daytime (3).

36   The letters before X L G M in the alphabet (4).

39   Second half of 'fool'. (2).

*40   The type of books that are about facts (3, 7).

45   Short for 'Reverend' (3).

*46   A story about lovers (7).

*48   The number of letters or numbers usually put on the back of a book by librarians (5).

50   What the 'T' stands for in T.V. (4).

*51   You can't talk _____ loud _____ you like (2).

52   Short for 'south-east' (2).

*53   Books with plays in (5).

54   The letters after D R K S in the alphabet (4).

Clues down

* 1   The person who writes a book (6).

2   Short for 'Edward' (3).

3   First two letters of 'oblong' (2).

* 4   Her job is in a library (9).

5   Liquid does this when it comes out slowly (4).

6   Consonants in the word 'gauge' (2).

7   Middle two letters of the word 'thirty' (2).

8   If you know how to do it you can find a book with _____ (4).

* 9   The section of the library about games and athletics (5).

10   A friendly way of saying goodbye (3, 3).

12   Short for 'Her Majesty' (2).

*14   Taking care (7).

*16   The name _____ the author (2).

21   Short for 'steam ship' (2).

22   Twenty hundredweights, or about a thousand kilogrammes (3).

24   When it hurts you feel this (4).

*26   A story that has been told for hundreds of years (4, 4).

27   Short for a 'pound' weight (2).

29   Short for 'direct current' electricity (2).

30   First two letters of 'etcetera' (2).

*31   You have to be _____ quiet (2).

*35   Types of books or stories (5).

36   Short for 'water closet' (2).

*37   What you pay for overdue books (5).

*38   A library that serves a particular district (5).

*40   To require or want (4).

41   If you keep a book too long they say it is _____ due (4).

*42   You can borrow a book _____ a library (4).

43   Letters before J P U B in the alphabet (4).

44   Birds build one to lay their eggs in (4).

45   Short for 'Rolls Royce' (2).

*47   'Catch *who* reading a book?' (2).

49   Short word used instead of a man's name (2).

14
Dialects

14.1 Children's games

Can you remember what the other kids said to you when you ran around in the Infant School?

Was it one of the words on this map?

Was it the word that the map shows for your district?

The people who made this map collected information from all over Britain about the words that 5-year olds and 6-year olds use.

Children don't learn these words from their parents. They learn them from each other. It's a sort of 'five-year-olds' English' that goes on year by year from small child to small child.

Head your work
14.1 Five-year olds' English

1 How many different words are shown on the map?
2 Which word is used in the biggest area?
3 Which words are a bit like another of the words?
4 Which of the words had you ever heard before?
5 Can you remember any other words of 'five-year-olds' English' from your own childhood, or hear any from small children living near you?

TO BE SURE, SHE'S FINE!

OCH, BUT SHE'S A BONNY LASS!

BOY! SHE'S A SMASHER!

LOOK YOU NOW, DID YOU EVER SEE ONE LIKE HER?

**Head your work
14.2 People who
talk dialect**

14.2 Local dialects

In chapter one we asked 'How many languages can you talk?' Now the question is: 'How many languages can you understand?'

People from different places speak in different ways. For them, it's ordinary English. *Yours* is the funny sort.

Each sort of English is called a dialect. A dialect can be shown by:
● how the vowels sound (the northern 'a' of 'castle' like 'cassel' — remember? Or the western 'Oi' for 'I').
● how the consonants sound (northerners make hard clicks with *d* and *t*, and still have a sound in their throats for -gh- in 'bright'.)
● how the sentence sounds (the Welsh and some Irish tend to say the sentence almost like a song).
● by the use of local words ('och', 'look you', 'our').
● by the order of the words.
● by which words are preferred — talking about *bonny* more often than *pretty*.

1   Do you know any people who use dialect on radio or television? If so, who are they and what are their dialects?

2   Who speaks dialect in your class or school? Which of the six points listed above do you notice in their speech?

3   Do you ever speak dialect yourself? If so, try to make a list of your 'local' words and phrases.

4   Do you like dialect? Which dialect forms (if any) do you particularly like — and are there some you really dislike?

14.3 Word match

**Head your work
14.3 Meanings of
dialect words**

The meanings of some dialect words may not be known to you. Put down what these words mean, and which dialect they belong to. You will find them in dictionaries, although not every word will be in every dictionary — you may have to look around through some different dictionaries to find them all.

bairn	ken	nowt
nobbut	wee	laird
mardy	colleen	kine

14.4   Recognizing different dialects

**Head your work
14.4   Key words in
different dialects
(Use sub-headings for
each dialect)**

Here is a collection of different forms of dialect English.
Find the key words or groups of words in each passage
that make it different from Standard Received English (the
type of English spoken by most announcers and news
readers on television and radio), and make lists of these
under the heading for that dialect.

If you can think of some more words to go in your lists for
each form, or some extra dialects to add, this will make
your work even more valuable.

West Country
Ah — and be ye! Well, I am truly glad to hear it, sir. I've
thought you mid do such a thing for some time. She's too
good for a dairymaid — I said so the very first day I zid
her — and a prize for any man; and what's more, a
wonderful woman for a gentleman-farmer's wife; he won't
be at the mercy of his baily wi' her at his side.

(Hardy — *Tess of the D'Urbervilles*)

Irish

'Shoor — a little bit of Heaven fell from out the sky one day! Eh, guv'nor, have yez a piece of paper I could be writin' on? That's dacent. It's me letter of resignation . . . Eh, I think I'll be havin' a drop to keep out the cold.'

(Garner — *Elidor*)

Scots

Ye flowery banks o' bonie Doon,
  How can ye blume sae fair?
How can ye chant, ye little birds,
  And I sae fu' o' care?

(Robert Burns)

Yorkshire

'Aye, Collinson's mill,' the Old Man says, grinning. He points. 'That one wi' t'biggest chimney o' t'lot.'
'It's not everybody's cup o' tea,' the Old Man admits.
'Some fowk like summat a bit . . . well, softer, if you know what I mean . . .'

(Barstow – *A Kind of Loving*)

Derbyshire

'Why, Your Ladyship's as welcome as Christmas ter th'hut an' th' key an' iverythink as is. On'y this time o' th' year there's bods ter set, an' Ah've got ter be potterin' abaht a good bit, seein' after 'em, an' a'. Winter time Ah ned 'ardly come nigh th' pleece.'

(D. H. Lawrence – *Lady Chatterley's Lover*)

Welsh

'But that was nothing to what things came out
From the sea-caves of Criccieth yonder.'
'What were they? Mermaids? dragons? ghosts?'
'Describe just one of them.'
                        'I am unable.'
'What were their colours?'
                        'Mostly nameless colours,
Colours you'd like to see.'

(Robert Graves – *Welsh Incident*)

Cockney

' 'Ullo! 'Ullo! Yes. This is Captain Dallas's'. No, it ain't the Captain – speakin' for 'im. No, 'e can't come 'isself. Why not? Cause if you must know 'e lost the use of 'is legs in a blow-up in the war – same time 'e found 'is V.C. See?'

(Clemence Dane – *Shivering Shocks*)

West African Pidgin

'You go remember Bafut, you go remember Bafut fine. Na for Bafut you done get plenty fine beef, no be so? When you go for your country, sometime you go tell your people de Fon of Bafut na your friend, an 'e done get you all dis fine beef, eh?'

(Gerald Durrell – *Bafut Beagles*)

14.5   A script for a play

**Head your work
14.5   Playscript
and a title**

Can you manage to speak some of these dialects well enough to be able to take a part in a play?
Can you manage to make a tape-recording using dialects – perhaps make your own 'radio play', with your own script?
Use tape-recorders to practice small parts. If you work in pairs you can help each other to get the sounds right.
It would be a good idea if your plot was one that brought in some travellers from different places, so that each member of your group spoke a different dialect.

Head your work
14.6   Write away!
(and the title)

14.6   Write away!

1   **'It's lovely to hear dialect spoken.'** Films wouldn't be much fun without them. What else would you miss if there wasn't dialect?

2   **United for the Cup!** Choose one of the First Division teams. Where have they played this year? What teams have they been against? Try to report their season with some imaginary conversations with their opponents speaking a few words of different dialects.

3   **The dialects I hear.** Which dialects do you hear spoken, who by, and what do they sound like? Write a separate short paragraph about each one.

14.7   Controversy

1   Children should not be brought up speaking dialect nowadays.
2   I'll speak as I want to speak and I don't care what anyone thinks.
3   Teachers don't help us enough to speak clearly – they seem to think we're too old to be helped.
4   Some dialects are good and some should not be allowed to continue – they are just lazy speech.
5   If we could all agree to talk the same way, we would all be much better friends. Dialects are leading to the breaking up of the United Kingdom.

14.8   Read all about it!

Have you ever heard of a home where the husband and wife swapped jobs for a day? The wife went out to do the husband's job and the husband had *all* (not just a few) of the daily home jobs to do.

Sean O'Casey has written a short play about this happening one day on a small Irish farm. The husband reckons the wife has an easy time in the home, so he is very happy when his friend Barry calls round for a chat. While they chat, things go wrong. The whole play is called *The End of the Beginning*.

How do you think it would turn out if a husband and wife you know swapped jobs? How would the baby and the pets get on? And would the car repairs get done? Can you make up a play or a story of your own along these lines? You will probably prefer not to try to write in dialect though.

Head your work
14.8   One man's meat
is another man's
poison

Riddle

What is broader than a Scottish loch?

An Irish shore (sure!).

14.9   Crossword number fourteen

Clues across

* 1   A midland county where D H Lawrence lived (10).
* 9   I am, she is, but you ___ (3).
  10   Many people call their grandmother this (4).
* 11   In this continent some speak Pidgin English (6).
  14   Three letters on the end of many words mean that whatever is happening keeps on happening (3).
  15   The letters after K K D B in the alphabet (4).
  16   This is found in the North Sea, together with oil (3).
  18   Short for 'Executive Officer' (2).
  19   The letters before S O I in the alphabet (3).

* 20   The dialect people speak in London (7).
* 24   We often write 'It's' instead of 'It ___' (2).
  25   Short for 'Technical Drawing' (2).
  26   It's made to be worn on a foot (4).
  27   What's left after a fire (3).

Clues down

* 1   A way of talking found in a particular part of the country (7).
* 2   Unusual or uncommon (such as hearing dialect on television) (4).
  3   Most houses in Britain are built of this material (5).
  4   The letters before Z F D in the alphabet (3).

  5   Consonants in the word 'huge' (2).
* 6   Dialect spoken in Ireland (5).
* 7   The small children went along very fast (3).
* 8   The language this book is about (7).
  12   Too much water in the wrong place (5).
* 13   To think the same as other people (5).
* 17   Could you remember ___ words of 'five-year old's English'? (3).
  21   Consonants in the word 'case' (2).
  22   The letters before L I in the alphabet (2).
* 23   The opposite of yes (2).
* 24   'I am', 'you are', but 'it ___' (2).

15
Corrections

Head your work
**15.1 Corrections
that are needed**

15.1 Proof reading

We've checked this book carefully so there aren't spelling mistakes or printing mistakes.

But we left part of this page for you to do. There are exactly 50 mistakes left in it. Can you find them? Note the line each mistake is on and also what the correction would be. You could make a chart using the headings given here:

Line no.	Mistake	Correction

By the way, the piece itself (from the book *High Wind in Jamaica*, by Richard Hughes), tells of the sort of wind that you can get in the tropics. If you think of the strongest wind you will ever have known in Britain, the wind you will be thinking of will be much less than a tropical storm of this type.

1 The wind by now saw more then redoubled. The sutters
2 were bulgeing as if tired elefants were leening against them,
3 and Father was trying to tye the fastening with that
4 hankerchief. But to push aganst this wind was lyke pushing
5 against rocke. The handkerchief, shutters, everithing berst;
6 the rain poored in like the see into a singking ship, the
7 wind occupied the roum, snatching picchers from the
8 wall, sweaping the table bear. Through the gaping frames
9 the lightning-lit sceen outside was vissible. The creepers,
10 witch befour had looked like codwebs, now streemed up
11 into the air like new-comed hair. Brushies were lying flatt,
12 laid bare on the grownd as close as a raddit lays back its
13 ears. Branches were leaping about lose in the sky. The
14 negro huts were clean gon, and the negroes crawling on
15 there stomacks across the compound to gain the shelter of
16 the houses. The bouncing rein seemed to covver the
17 ground with a white smoak, a sort of sea in which the
18 local people wallowed like porpoises. One negro boy
19 began to role away; his mother, forgeting caution, rose to
20 her feet; and immediately, the fat old lady was blown cleen
21 away, bowling along ackross fields and hedgerows like
22 someone in a funy fairy-storey, till she fetched up aggainst
23 a wall and wos pined their, unnable to move.

15.2 How many 'mistakes' are slips?

Everybody makes some spelling mistakes.
We make most mistakes when we are tired, or in a hurry, or not thinking what we are doing.
Most of these mistakes are slips.
Silly little mistakes that we know are wrong.

Only we never noticed we had made the mistakes.
That is why it is useful to get in the habit of checking your work through.

1   How many of your own mistakes are slips? Bring in a long piece of writing you've done in another lesson – best of all, some writing where you were putting things down in your own way.
Check it through yourself to see how many spelling mistakes you can find.

Make a list of them like this:

Line no.	Mistake	Correction	Did I really know the right spelling?

2   Next ask someone else to check the same work for any mistakes you missed. It may be useful to have a dictionary handy for checking up words you are not sure about. Add these words to the list.

3   Do the same thing with the punctuation marks in the piece.

4   How many of your mistakes were slips? ___ out of a total of ___ mistakes.

For most people, cutting out the slips is half the battle with spelling.

15.3   Word match

Use a dictionary if you need it to correct the slips in these rather more difficult words. In each case at least the first three letters are right.

Wrong spellings

1   assissant
2   busness
3   certificut
4   chockolate
5   cuppoard
6   emploiment
7   engineating
8   Febuary
9   intrested
10   laboratry

11   libary
12   offiss
13   personell (manager)
14   picher (to look at)
15   rasberry
16   secretery
17   seperate
18   secondry
19   tecknickle
20   vacansies

15.4   Making a fair copy

There will be times when you want to write something without any mistakes at all.

It might be when you have to write for a job.
It might be that you want to write to a newspaper.
The best way then is to make a **draft**.
Then you check the draft and make your corrections on it.
Then you make a fair copy.

1   Here is a draft letter for a newspaper. Make your own fair copy of it. Lay it out carefully on paper that would do for a letter.

2   When you have done this, see if you can make a draft of a letter of your own. Then check it. And make a fair copy.
You might like to write your letter about jobs people ought to find for 16-year olds, or about bad roads, or parking places, or about a shortage of playing fields, or swimming baths — or what you like.

```
                                        Flat 78,
                                                   s
                                        Hilltop Manⱡions

                                        Newcaⱡstⱡle
June 14th


Dear s̶i̶r̶, Sir,


Near where                                              c
N̶e̶r̶e̶ w̶e̶r̶e̶ I live there are lots of stray dogs around. I was shoⱡked
                    patrol
when I saw the dog p̶e̶t̶r̶o̶l̶e̶ van/come round the other day and take ⱡall
                          said     would   killed          owners
these dogs away. The man s̶e̶d̶  they w̶o̶o̶d̶ be k̶i̶l̶d̶   if the o̶n̶e̶r̶s̶

did not come and collect them this week.
                                        who    would
        There must be lots of teenagers like me h̶o̶w̶  w̶o̶o̶d̶  love to help
                                                        Can't
look after these dogs, and we could pay for their food. C̶a̶r̶n̶'̶t̶ the
council                  dogs'
c̶o̶u̶n̶s̶i̶l̶ make a sort of d̶o̶g̶s̶ home where we could go and see them?


                        sincerely
            Yours s̶i̶n̶s̶e̶r̶

                Helen Barker

            Helen Barker
```

15.5 Correcting a typescript

Someone may type something for you one day.
It might be for a class magazine. Who edits it?
It might be for a club you belong to.
It might be at work.
And there might be mistakes in it. You will need to get rid of them.
There are ways of marking these mistakes that everybody will understand.

Here is the code:

s /= cross out this letter and put *s* (or whatever it should be) instead.

⊙ /= put in a full stop that is missing.

caps/= make this letter a big one. (Upper case)

lc /= make this letter a small one. (Lower case)

⌒ /= join up this word that has fallen apart.

/= space out these words that have stuck together.

ઈ /= rub this out.

Head your work
15.5 Correcting a typescript

Now make a list of corrections for the typescript below, using this code. The first two mistakes are marked for you. You should be able to find 10 more mistakes.
Set it out like this:

Line no.	Mistake	Code	What correct form should be
1	words stuck	# /	next thing
2	e left out	e /	switched

```
 1.   The nextthing was that Mr. Boss went over and

 2.   switchd the machine on.  There was a bang and a

 3.   cloud of blue smoke.  I could not see where

 4.   Mr. Boss had gone later I found him upside down

 5.   in the bind marked 'rubbish'.  He waswhite with

 6.   an ger.  He shouted at me from the bin: 'Why the

 7.   hell did you do that?' SHe seemed to Think I had

 8.   done it on purpose.  There was still a lot of blue

 9.   smoke around.  Just then Mr. Peace came by.  'Is

10.   there anything wrong?' he usked. 'Have you seen Mr.

11.   Boss anyw here?'  'His Feet are over there,' I said.
```

15.6 Write away!

Head your work
15.6 Write away!
(and the title)

Remember to check your work through to make sure there are no slips. You may want to do a fair copy later.

1 **My pet _____.** The life history of a pet you have got now, or have had in the past.

2 **A wonderful day.** Describe a really happy day — perhaps on holiday, or at home, or at school. Was it a surprising thing that happened, or a plan that worked out right?

3 **Fools on the road.** What makes you 'see red' when you are travelling? Is it other drivers, pedestrians, animals, or the police? Tell some stories of things that have made you cross.

15.7 Controversy

Head your work
15.7 Controversy
about daily issues

1 There's too much American music around these days. All the best Groups are British.
2 People make too much fuss about hooligans at football matches. Everyone enjoys watching the game.
3 We should not be allowed to wear exactly what we like at school, because one works best if one is a bit 'dressed up'.
4 People can get guns and air rifles far too easily. They shouldn't be sold in shops at all.
5 The way people look after their pets is dreadful.

111

15.8 Read all about it

Head your work
15.8 (and the title
of your poem)

Do you like modern verse — the sort that doesn't rhyme
and where the lines vary in length? Often there are several
layers of meaning to dig for too — some of the key words
may mean what they seem to mean, and at the same time
may stand for something quite different. Try your hand at
writing some. Here is an example.

People
I like people quite well
at a little distance.
I like to see them passing and passing
and going their own way,
especially if I see their aloneness alive in them.
Yet I don't want them to come near.
If they will only leave me alone
I can still have the illusion that there is room enough
in the world.

D H Lawrence

15.9 Crossword number fifteen

Clues across

* 1   A piece of paper that says that you have managed to do something, like passing an exam (11).
10   A girl's name that is also the name of a colour rather like green (5).
12   We choose our representatives by _____ for them (6).
*14   The colour of traffic lights to stop you (3).
*15   To use a machine to write your words (4).
16   First two letters of the word 'gunwale' (2).
17   Short for 'Road' on an address (2).
19   Come first in a race (3).
20   The place where an ambassador works (7).
*26   Brown bars that are good to eat (9).
28   The letters before F K in the alphabet (2).
30   The most important part, that is the basis of all the rest (5).
*32   A thought in your head (4).
33   First half of the word 'Indian' (3).
34   Your brother's son (6).
36   Consonants in the word 'room' (2).
37   The letters before Z D F T U in the alphabet (5).
38   Girl's name made from the first five letters of 'ladies' (5).
40   Short for 'Linda' (3).
41   A small two-piece garment worn by ladies on the beech (6).
42   Vowels in the word 'tame' (2).
44   The letters before T H D in the alphabet (3).
*45   Very big and expensive houses (8).

Clues down

* 1   Putting something right (10).
* 2   When you remove a mistake you get _____ of it (3).
3   Short for 'television' (2).
4   It means 'that is', although these two letters really stand for the Latin words 'id est' (2).
5   A green plant that climbs up trees (3).
* 6   Something written out for the second time (4).
7   Last three letters of the word 'certificate' (3).
8   First half of the word 'tiny' (2).
* 9   Working with making engines or big machines (11).
11   A horse can be _____ by its bridle (3).
*13   You can shoot with it (3).
*18   Taking on new workers would be filling these (9).
21   The letters before N I in the alphabet (2).
22   Famous pop singer who sings many modern songs (3, 5).
23   First half of the word 'some' (2).
*24   Accidental little mistakes (5).
25   A type of sailing boat (5).
27   The letters before F J X F L in the alphabet (5).
*29   An island in the West Indies (7).
31   Noticed or observed (4).
*35   When someone puts a magazine or a newspaper together, he _____ it (5).
*39   Words in a column (4).
43   Last half of the word 'also' (2).

16
When English is your second language

16.1 Mix-up

True story:
French teacher to a class of pupils learning English:

Teacher: 'In what circumstances does an Englishman wear his cudgel?'

Pupils: 'We know not.'

Teacher: 'When he goes for a walk with his dog.'

Explanation: The teacher used 'wear' instead of 'carry'; and he used 'cudgel' instead of 'walking stick'. He had found these words in his dictionary.

Swedish visitor faced with a problem:
'I'll look at it from all angels.'
What did he mean to say? How did his mistake arise?

Head your work
16.1 Do dictionaries give the right word?

1 Find some dictionaries for other languages and look up the English meanings given for these foreign words. Set out your answers like this:

French		German		Swedish		Latin	
word	translation	word	translation	word	translation	word	translation
poisson		Fisch		fisc		piscis	
maison		Haus		bolig		domus	
gateau		Kuchen		kake		placenta	
fromage		Kase		ost		caseus	
arbre		Baum		träd		arbor	

2 Did you find all these words had the same meaning in English? What variations did you find?

3 Try to collect information about what these five things mentioned in question 1 are like in each of these countries. Are they the same in each place?

16.2 Be an explorer: Can you cope with the language?

1   What is Marty the Martian talking about here? Put down what you think is being said.
2   What did some others in the class think was being said here? Did you all think it was the same thing, or could some of you be making mistakes – *mis*-understanding?
3   Think of a misunderstanding that could have led to a quarrel between people speaking different languages – perhaps between Marty the Martian and the commissionaire in the pictures here.

16.3   Word match

When two words mean exactly the same thing they are called *synonyms*. 'Car' and 'automobile' are synonyms.

One of the things that makes translation difficult is that a word in one language is hardly ever a synonym for a word in another. The French word 'main' *is* a synonym for the English 'hand', but the French word 'petit déjeuner' does not mean a meal quite like our 'breakfast'.

Look at this list of pairs of English words. Which ones of these are synonyms? For the ones that are not synonyms, explain what the differences are.

1   a radio, a wireless
2   a jersey, a jumper
3   white, colourless
4   warm, mild
5   a photo, a picture
6   a pony, a foal
7   a donkey, an ass
8   a fungus, a toadstool
9   a rally, a race
10   football, soccer.

16.4   Missing words

Translating from one language to another is not always easy. There may not be a word in the other language for the word you want to translate. Or there may be several different words and you have to choose between them.

Norwegian is a language which is very much like English. Many of the words are similar. But even so you would find it difficult to translate the simple word 'no'.

JEG HAR INGEN
PENGER.

English	Norwegian
No, thank you.	*Nei* takk.
I have *no* money.	Jeg har *ingen* penger.
*No*body came.	*Ingen* kom.
No more.	*Ikke* mer.

You would also have problems with 'please':

English	Norwegian
Please sit down.	*Værsågod* sitt.
No smoking *please*.	*Vennligst* ikke røke.
Yes *please*.	Ja *takk*.
Please yourself.	Gjør *hva du vil*.

1   Make a list of the Norwegian words for 'no' and for 'please'.

2   Here are three Norwegian words with illustrations to show what they mean. Can you think of ONE English word for each one – and if not, what do you need to say?

Explanations of these three words are on page 139.

3   When you have answered questions **1** and **2** can you explain why a dictionary is not enough on its own to help you translate from one language to another?

16.5   Our funny language

There are a lot of things we say in our language that are not very easy to translate into another language. Look at each of the sentences below and write down *two* things about them:

a) what they really mean

b) what someone who hasn't learnt English well might think they mean, by mistake.

1   It's raining cats and dogs.
2   To hear it from the horse's mouth.
3   To take it lying down.
4   To miss it by the skin of your teeth.
5   To be stumped.
6   To do a ton up.
7   To be as fit as a fiddle.
8   To have a fit of the blues.

16.6 Write away

Head your work
16.6 Write away!
(and the title)

1 **The people on the bus.** Have you travelled on a bus and heard people chattering away in some other language that you could not understand at all? What did it sound like? What special sounds could you catch? Could you get any idea of what they were saying? Try to make up a story that starts with people in a bus talking in a foreign language. What does it lead to after you get off?

2 **Difficult English.** Interview someone who has had to learn English as a foreign language. What did he or she find most difficult about learning it? How did he or she manage to learn it? Does he need your help to learn more?

3 **Languages spoken near my home.** Make a survey of the languages spoken near your home – what are they, what languages are they similar to, and who speaks them? What are the numbers 1–10 in each of these languages?

16.7 Controversy

Head your work
16.7 Controversy
about language

1 The whole world ought to speak the same language.
2 We all ought to learn to speak a foreign language properly.
3 Some people exploit the people who need to learn English by charging much too much for bad lessons.
4 Newspapers in Britain ought to have some columns printed in foreign languages.
5 Welsh, Irish and Scotsmen should make a point of speaking their own languages rather than English. They should take a pride in their countries.

16.8 Read all about it

Gerald Durrell has travelled all over the world collecting animals for zoos. He has written about his journeys in a series of books that all make good reading. His journey to Bafut in West Africa is described in *The Bafut Beagles*.

One of the things that makes all his books lively is the way he tells his conversations with the local people – and of course, there is often a lot of difficulty with speaking English. You would find a lot of fun in his books.

Head your work
16.8 Strange
encounter

Perhaps you can try your hand at telling a lively story of a strange encounter you could imagine? Perhaps you are out looking for rabbits in the country, and a stranger comes by and chats away? Or you are down by the docks, when a sailor from abroad begins to talk?

Clues across

* 1 The language the ancient Romans used to talk (5).
* 5 The part of Africa where Gerald Durrell collected zoo animals (5).
  10 A very long time (4).
*12 A man whose job is going to sea (6).
*13 A country in Scandinavia that goes far to the North (6).
  16 Short for 'Mother' (2).
*17 The language spoken in Germany (6).
*18 You can miss something by this much of your teeth (4).
  20 You and me (2).
*21 Difficulties (8).
  23 Small winding roads in the countryside (5).
  25 First half of the word 'plot' (2).
  26 Carefully, and kindly perhaps? (6).

  29 Short for 'alternating current' (2).
  31 When there is no wind (4).
  32 To spend time until something happens or someone comes (4).
*34 An account of what happened (5).
*35 If you get it from this creature's mouth, what you hear should be right (5).

Clues down

* 1 Different words and different ways of saying things in different countries (9).
  2 A very short word meaning just one (1).
  3 First half of the word 'terrific' (4).
  4 A common word found in 'this' (2).
  5 Short for 'Bachelor of Arts' degree (2).
  6 Points or directs towards (4).
  7 A flat little piece shaved off (5).

  8 Vowels in the word 'duo' (2).
* 9 To change from one language to another (9).
  11 If I go, she _____ (4).
*12 A word that means the same as another word (7).
  14 Letters after V L O K in the alphabet (4).
*15 A meeting of a lot of cars organised by the Automobile Association (1, 1, 5).
  19 A cheeky little fellow (3).
  22 Common word found in 'been' (2).
  24 To cut with a big-toothed blade (3).
  27 Short for 'Non-commissioned Officer' (3).
  28 Sticky black material used for roads (3).
*30 A synonym for 'automobile' (3).
  33 I am, you are, he _____ (2).

17
Out at work

Save our milkmen

'After ten days talking to milk companies throughout the United States, we're sure of one thing—the doorstep milk delivery service must be maintained to ensure continued job security.

'In England and Wales, 90,000 workers are involved, approximately 45,000 in deliveries alone and, of these, over 10,000 in the London area. Ninety-two per cent of homes in England and Wales have milk delivered to the door. But, in America, doorstep delivery is now almost non-existent—88 per cent of milk is sold through retail outlets.

'If doorstep delivery diminished in this country the escalation of the numbers of people out of work would be rapid throughout the industry. Thousands would lose their jobs.

'The motivation in the industry is very different here from in the States. Here we do provide a unique service to the customer; one which the customer needs and relies on. It is this service element that gives job satisfaction to many who work in the distributive side of the industry.

'The franchise system now operates widely in the States for both the remaining small percentage of home deliveries and for some of those to shops and supermarkets. There is no basic wage. Men must purchase their van, tyres, petrol, products, etc, from the milk company—and in some states, we saw vehicles eaten with rust, tyres worn smooth, that wouldn't be allowed in this country.

'There is no service, no relief system to cover the franchise man when he is off work. And so his round diminishes. In some states, where local laws allowed people to work any hours out of the twenty-four, the average working day started at four a.m. and went on until three or four p.m. Shops were open 18 to 24 hours a day and deliveries had to be made at a time to suit the shopkeeper, no matter what time of the day or night that was.

'Maintaining a sensible price control here is one of the things everyone in the industry should support to keep consumption high and doorstep delivery secure.

'It was the big price-cutting war in the mid 'fifties that put half the U.S. dairies out of business and sent doorstep deliveries and liquid milk consumption down the drain.

'Milk, sold through the supermarkets as a "loss leader", lured custom from the doorstep and killed jobs. Neither did it generate any increase in jobs in the supermarkets. Automation and simplification in packaging has completed the reduction of jobs throughout the entire industry.

'We saw a lot in America which led to the decline of the doorstep delivery. "Be your own boss", the myth they promote and the workers accept, sounds fine—but if you don't make it, you're out!

'We must ensure that those mistakes are not repeated here.'

17.1 Save our milkmen!

1   Where did the writers go to find out about where milk is sold?
2   How many workers have jobs to do with delivery milk?
3   How many workers are actually out on the rounds?
4   How do most people in America get their milk?
5   Why do British milkmen find their job satisfying?
6   Why are American milkmen rather like British ice-cream van drivers?
7   What do the American franchise milkmen have to buy?
8   What happens to his round when an American franchise milkman is off work through sickness?
9   Why does the American franchise milkman have to work long hours?
10   What made Americans stop having milk deliveries?
11   How did the supermarkets persuade Americans to carry heavy bottles of milk home?
12   Did the supermarkets need more staff when they started selling a lot of milk?
13   Why are there fewer jobs now in the whole American milk industry?
14   How did the Americans persuade milkmen to accept the franchise system?
15   Did the authors discuss whether it mattered if the housewife got her milk as cheaply as possible or not?

17.2 Your secret message

You're sent on a special mission.
You have to get some secret information.
You will have to send it on a piece of paper that you are going to hide in something very small.
How brief can you make your notes, and yet say everything? Use the milkman piece (17.1) for practice.
The questions in 17.1 guide you to the most important points.
What you are asked to do is to make a report, not to answer questions.
But your report can have little words left out.
The material covered by the first 6 questions is done to start you off.
Write this out and try to finish the whole report in about 50 more words. You can change the order of the information if you like.

Visited America. 90,000 British workers distribute milk, half on deliveries. 88% American milk sold in shops. British milkmen like helping people. Americans use franchise system. Must buy . . .

17.3 Word match

Head your work
**17.3 Words from a
Trade Union paper**

There were a lot of words in the piece about the milkmen that need quite a bit of explaining. Can you explain them? The dictionary may not help you with the ones with a star *. Explanations for these are given below the list.

maintained   unique
security   distributive
*retail outlets   *loss leader
diminished   automation
*escalation   myth
motivation   *franchise

* Two words in the list that mean shops, supermarkets, hypermarkets, and street stalls.
* A long word that means getting higher and higher (like the steps on an escalator).
* A word that means having permission, or a licence, to do a particular job in a particular area.
* Something sold at less than it cost, so that more customers want to come to the shop.

17.4 Notes from someone talking

There will be many times when you may need to make notes while someone is talking.
● At Technical Colleges many of the teachers give a 'lecture' rather than make it like a class lesson in school. They may put some notes on the board but they will expect you to add points of your own while they talk.
● Your employer may send you on a course like that too.
● If you are interested in Union work, the Union will also arrange courses where they expect you to take notes.

To do it well needs practice.

- You must write key words, not sentences.
- Shorten long words.
- You must listen while you are writing.
- You must try to pick out the important points – like the key words in a paragraph (see p. 34).
- **Don't** try to write down everything said – it is not possible unless you are brilliant at short-hand.

(see p. 34)

Head your work
17.4 Paul's notes while someone was talking

Here is a short piece and some notes Paul made on it.

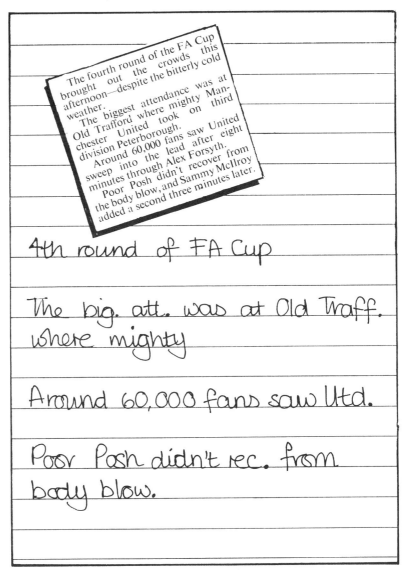

The fourth round of the FA Cup brought out the crowds this afternoon—despite the bitterly cold weather.

The biggest attendance was at Old Trafford where mighty Manchester United took on third division Peterborough.

Around 60,000 fans saw United sweep into the lead after eight minutes through Alex Forsyth. Poor Posh didn't recover from the body blow, and Sammy McIlroy added a second three minutes later.

4th round of FA Cup

The big. att. was at Old Traff. where mighty

Around 60,000 fans saw Utd.

Poor Posh didn't rec. from body blow.

1 Which of the 5 'rules' above has Paul forgotten?
2 Which of the 5 'rules' has Paul used?
3 Did Paul's notes make good sense?
4 Can you make better notes from the same passage? Have a go!

17.5 Making your own notes

Head your work
17.5 My own notes

Try some more practice at making notes.
Work in pairs.
One reads out one of these pieces fairly slowly, but not waiting specially while the other writes.
The other makes notes.
Then swap round and work on the next piece.
When you have finished mark each other's work.

- Do the notes make sense?
- Do the notes pick out the 4 most important facts?
- Did your partner keep up?
- How many of the 5 key 'rules' (see 17.4) have been obeyed?

Cricket pitches too small

Why don't the cricket authorities admit that we have grown too big for traditional cricket dimensions? When the present 22-yard pitch was first chosen in around 1700, the average man was 5 ft 4½ ins tall; now he is 5 ft 9 ins. Moreover, the speed of bowling has probably grown even more; for example, the mile is now run 15 per cent faster than a century ago. Some other sports have faced the physical facts of modern life. In the late 1940s, for instance, Eton school had finally to enlarge their traditional boats to accommodate the larger bottoms of ever-growing Eton schoolboys.

Looking after cats

Bad teeth Dribbling in cats is often caused by a layer of yellow tartar on the teeth, which also causes inflammation of the gums. Very few people seem to realize that cats do suffer with bad teeth, and a vet will remove these and also any yellow tartar.

Bites and stings A bite or scratch from another cat in a fight often turns into an abscess or a sore. Any such bites or scratches should be bathed as soon as noticed with a mild disinfectant.

Cats may be stung through pawing at bees or wasps. A bee sting should be removed with a pair of tweezers and the place dabbed with bicarbonate of soda mixed in water.

Tar on feet When road repairs are in progress, the cat's feet may become covered with tar. The cat must not be allowed to lick it off, as it is a poison. Wipe off as much as possible, and cover the pads with butter.

17.6 Write away!

Head your work
17.6 Write away!
(and the title)

1 **Useful jobs.** Which jobs in the community do you think are useful, and what do you like about them? Milkman, postman, policeman, traffic warden, teacher, librarian, nurse, doctor, council clerk, dustman, parks gardener, bricklayer, meter-reader — or any other?

2 **What I think America must be like.** Have you got any pictures to put in? What have you heard about it, read about it or seen on film? Have you ever been there? Would you like to live there? Why — or why not?

3 **Me, the great spy.** A really imaginative story of a mission you were sent on, and how you accomplished it — what dangers you faced and what brilliant ideas you had. (Ever seen a spy film?)

17.7 Controversy

Head your work
17.7 Controversy
about bothering

1 It's silly to waste people's time with fetching milk from a shop.
2 It's silly having separate deliveries for milk, post, and papers to the same house.
3 Why bother with making notes? I'll take the cassette along.
4 Notes don't help me remember anything. I remember programmes from telly OK without them.
5 Work in the old days must have been much nicer than it is now — milkmen had horses, and clerks could do their writing by hand.

17.8 Read all about it

Many of the coloured people living in the United States are poor, and have badly paid jobs. Until recent years they were often not allowed to send their children to the same schools as white children, or to sit in the same part of the bus as white people. Some of the coloured people wanted to fight for these rights with guns and bombs. But one of their leaders, Martin Luther King, convinced them that it was better to use persuasion. The fact that the coloured people now have won these rights proves that Martin Luther King's approach was right, but he made enemies for himself. In the end he was shot and killed when he was going to one of his big meetings.

The story of his life and work is told by his wife in a book called *My Life with Martin Luther King*. One of the things the book shows is how much importance a leader can have when he sets about trying to persuade people to change their minds.

Head your work
17.8 (and your own title)

In her book Mrs Coretta King tells about the telephone call she had when her husband was shot. Can you write about the most terrible, or most exciting, moment that has happened in your own life? Or, if you feel you have never had anything very special happen, perhaps you could imagine a time when something might happen, and how you would feel about it?

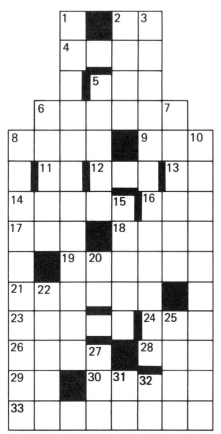

17.9 Crossword number seventeen

Clues across

2 A short way to say 'What did you say?' (2).

4 What you might call a friend whose real name is Andrew (4).

5 To drink a small amount (3).

6 In better condition (you might say this about an athlete, for example) (6).

8 As well as (4).

9 The usual name for a Representative of a firm (3).

*11 A short word that means 'whether' (2).

12 The name for a male sheep (3).

13 First half of the word 'team' (2).

14 A man who wanders from place to place, with no steady job or home (5).

16 Second half of the word 'bazaar' (3).

17 Short for 'Officers Training Corps' (3).

18 A boy's name that can be made with the same letters as are in the word 'rice' (4).

19 The noise made by a small bell (6).

*21 It'll be easy – It'll be '__ ____ of cake' (1, 5).

23 Not these, but ____ (5).

24 Short for the explosive of which the full name is 'tri nitro-toluene' (3).

26 You may have used this word in science when talking about electrons that had, or did not have, charges (4).

28 Middle of the word 'persuaded' (3).

29 Short for 'Old Testament' (2)

30 '____' to the bad weather the match has been cancelled (5).

33 Things that are not sense at all (8).

Clues down

*1 A feeling of being satisfied (12).

2 An editor will do this (to a book, magazine or newspaper) (4).

*3 Specially large sorts of supermarkets that people may drive miles to go to (12).

5 Very bad weather, sometimes with thunder and lightning (5).

6 What a girl who is teasing a boy might be called (5).

*7 To sell to the public (6).

*8 Making machines do the work for the people (10).

*10 The amount of a hundred parts (10).

15 More than one penny (5).

20 It stands for 'that is', although the actual words it stands for are the Latin words 'id est' (2).

22 A picture made with a camera (5).

25 Women who lead a religious life (4).

27 Message sent from a sinking ship (3).

31 You and I (2).

32 A shorter way to say 'inside' (2).

18
Children talking

18.1 Are small children care-free?

Now as I was young and easy under the apple boughs
About the lilting house and happy as the grass was green,
   The night above the dingle starry,
    Time let me hail and climb
   Golden in the heydays of his eyes . . .

Heaven lies about us in our infancy!
Shades of the prison-house begin to close
   Upon the growing Boy . . .

1   Do you know any young children well? — Brothers and sisters, nephews and nieces, ones you baby-sit for? How old are they?
2   Do the really small children you know (or the ones your friends know) usually seem to be 'young and easy — happy as the day is long'?
3   If you know any small children who do not seem very happy, do you know any reason why they are unhappy?
4   What worries have pupils of secondary-school age that small children do not usually have?
5   Do you think the pieces from the poems at the top of this page fit with childhood? If not, which bits are wrong, and why?

18.2   Learning to talk

How much can you say without words?
Are you good at mime?
Can you mime some ideas for the class to guess?
Try and see.

You'll probably mime things like:

| eating | laughing | fighting |
| drinking | crying | helping |

It's not so easy to mime things like:
'I think we all ought to stop school at 3.30 p.m.'
'The best metal to use for this part of the engine is . . .'
'I want the forwards to attack on the left wing.'

That means that one can live without words.
But one cannot live well without plenty of words.
(Ever tried thinking without words?)
Learning words begins soon after we are born.
The most important part of learning words is done before a child goes to school. The most important teachers are the parents and friends — perhaps you.

1   What words do very small children learn first?
2   Make a list between you of words you know *children under two* use.
3   How many of the words on your list are nouns ('naming' words)?
4   How many of the words on your list are verbs ('doing' words)?
5   How many other words are there, which are neither nouns nor verbs?

Children learn nouns first because they can see and touch the things they are talking about. They can see or feel what happens with verbs so these come next.

First they must talk about things they can see and touch for a long time. Then they can begin to talk about things that aren't there but that they could see and touch if they were. Lastly they can begin to talk about things no-one can see: ideas, qualities like fear or courage, and things or events that are made up.

Think of how small children spend their days.

6　What do you think are the 20 most important nouns for a small child to understand?

7　What do you think are the 10 most important verbs for a small child to understand?

18.3　Word match

**Head your work
18.3　Concrete and abstract nouns**

1　Which of these nouns are 'concrete', which means they are about things you can see, touch, hear, taste, or smell; and which are 'abstract', which means they are about ideas, things you can never sense (see, touch, hear, taste, smell)?

bread　thread　weather　ignorance　leather　amusement feather　silence　obedience　heather　arrangement engagement

2　Which group of these words will small children find difficult to understand or use?

18.4　Reading to children

There are hundreds of good books for small children. Have a look at some of them to see how the words are used. Perhaps you can each borrow one or two and bring them in to look at together?

Some of the many good ones are books by the following authors:

Joan Robinson
Dorothy Edwards
Russell Hoban
A. A. Milne
Inger and Lasse Sandberg
Sheila McCullach

If you can look at some of these good ones, you will see the words fit well with how children talk. They amuse small children, and at the same time help them to learn new words.

You may also find some well-known books in your collection that do not use words in the same way. The words seem stiff and strange, even if they are easy words.

**Head your work
18.4　Good books for children**

When you have looked through the books, make notes about the three you think are best, and say what you like about them; and about the three you think are not so good for small children, and why they are not.

Best of all, try reading one or two of these stories to small children.

Points to look for:

easy for small children	hard for small children
concrete nouns	abstract nouns
a setting they can recognise	a completely strange setting
children or animals they think are like themselves	no-one to 'pretend to be me'
an interesting or funny story	boring story
lively words like children use	stiff, grown-up language

18.5 How long can one word last?

How many words do you use in a minute? Perhaps two of you could have a lively chat, and one check the time for a minute, while the fourth in the group counts how many words are spoken.

Now see if you can get a chance this evening to count how many words a small child will use — if he or she will keep talking for a minute. You are likely to find it is a much smaller number. The child is still finding it difficult to make the sounds in a word; each word can last a long time.

**Head your work
18.5   Speeds of
talking**

1   Why do you need a lot of patience when talking to small children?
2   How fast do you think you should talk to small children when you are explaining something new?
3   What would be the best way of teaching a small child a new word?
4   What else does a child need to learn besides nouns and verbs? What colours? Left and right? Words about 'when' — past, present and future? What else can you think of?
5   How can people make sure that small children have enough time for talking every day? How much talking time do you think they might need (depending, of course, on age)?

18.6　Write away!

**Head your work
18.6　Write away!
(and the title)**

1　**Funny stories about babies.** Stories you have heard about things babies or small children say or do; funny scrapes they have got into, funny things they have said.

2　**A story for children.** Have you a younger brother or sister that you read to? Has he or she a 'favourite' book? What is it about? Do you enjoy it too?

3　**Good toys for children.** What were the toys that mattered most to you when you were young? What do small children seem to play with most now? How do they use these toys? Do they learn a lot from them?

18.7　Controversy

**Head your work
18.7　Controversy
about small
children**

1　All children should be sent to a playgroup or a nursery school by the time they are four.
2　Mums ought not to go to work until their children start school – they (or the dads) should be at home with the children.
3　Fathers ought to spend at least as much time with the children as mothers do.
4　Five is too young to start school. In most countries children do not begin until six or even seven.
6　Small children should spend a lot of time with their grandparents.

18.8　Read all about it!

A. A. Milne wrote the 'Christopher Robin' stories and poems a long time ago. They remain enormously popular. One of the very clever things about them is that he has been able to amuse both the adult who is reading the story and the child at the same time – but with different jokes. While the child is laughing at something he finds funny, the adult can laugh at something the child would never understand.

See how many of the Christopher Robin stories and poems you can read.

Try your hand at writing for small children. Can you think of some more adventures for the family of animals that Christopher Robin lives with?

**Head your work
18.8　Pooh's at it
again**

Riddle
When can it be good to be 'on the bottle' and be a heavy drinker?

When you're a baby.

18.9 Crossword number eighteen

Clues across

* 1 A time when you are a child (9).
 9 Many children's stories start '_____ upon a time' (4).
 10 Another word for 'baby' – there were two in the wood in a fairy story (4).
 11 Vowels in the word 'stream' (2).
* 12 The sort of word that tells us about doing something (4).
 14 Taken in your hand from one place to another (7).
 16 First half of the word 'ants' (2).
* 17 To act without words (4).
* 19 Having your food (6).
 22 A long period of years (3).
 23 Consonants in the word 'tune' (2).
* 24 The sort of word that tells us the name of things (4).
 25 Animals often kept as pets (4).
 27 Short for 'company' (2).
 29 Consonants in the word 'your' (2).
* 30 Each one, all of them (5).

Clues down

* 1 Hard and solid – even a noun can be like this (8).
 2 The letters after G M in the alphabet (2).
 3 Frozen water (3).
* 4 Getting to know (8).
 5 Consonants in the word 'daub' (2).
* 6 When you've got something you _____ it (4).
* 7 Doing what you are told (9).
 8 A poetic word meaning 'over' (3).
* 13 It's made from flour, and we usually eat it cold (5).
 15 Animal with a long tail (3).
 17 Letters before N H V in the alphabet (3).
 18 Short for 'mister' (2).
 20 _____ Pandy has a set of children's books about himself (4).
 21 You breathe through it (4).
 26 Second half of 'door' (2).
 28 A small word for choosing between things (2).

19
Explain yourself

**Head your work
19.1   Things I can
do well**

19.1   Clever out of school

Lots of people can do well when they are out of school.
It's only in school where they never get very far. And some
lucky ones can do well IN school as well as OUT of school.

1   Are there any things in the list below that *you* can do
well?
2   A good way of knowing if you can do something well
is to think how often people ask you about it, or ask you
to do it for them.
How many other things of the same type can you do well?
3   Are you an 'in school', 'out of school' or 'bit of both'
type?

Examples of in-school things
Help librarian tidy up books
Play in a games team
Play chess
Draw good pictures
Paint well
Make things of wood or metal
Bake, boil, or fry well
Care for animals in Biology or Rural Science lab.
Play guitar, drums, wind instrument
Act or sing well in a play
Make up good stories or poems
Write tidily and clearly
Do sums accurately
Draw well in Technical Drawing
Do good topic work
(What else?)

Examples of out-of-school things
Change a baby's nappy or baby sit
Repair a motor bike
Ride in a cycling club
Ride a horse or pony
Know almost every breed of dog
Catch almost any sort of fish
Know the star constellations and planets
Grow vegetables successfully
Tidy a flower garden
Redecorate a room or build a wall
Take photographs
Sing a lot of pop songs
Belong to a Group
Keep a part-time job as long as you want it.
Watch wild birds or keep budgerigars
(What else?)

19.2   Get them interested!

Often there's a problem about something you can do well. That is – no one ever seems to get interested in it. You may be an expert on the foot diseases of earwigs, but whenever you mention it to your friends they just scream, or giggle, or say 'Really?' and talk about something else.

You just can't get them talking about earwigs.

And that's no good in interviews, or when meeting visitors, and at times like that.

So how do you make things interesting?

Let's think about your school.

If you've had four or five years there, it probably seems ordinary to you now. Just school. Just what you expect school to be. How can you talk about it if someone says 'Tell me about your school'?
- How big is it? (Schools vary a lot in size).
- Is it for boys *and* girls? (Some are and some are not.)
- How far do pupils come each day? (Some need buses and others don't.)
- Which is its best team just now, and how have they got on?
- What clubs are there? Do any of the clubs:
  hold interesting meetings?
  put on displays?
  win competitions?
- What do you enjoy doing most in the school?
- Are there any special facts, or buildings, or rooms in the school?

**Head your work
19.2   Selling your
interest**

1   Make *notes* in answer to these questions about your school.
2   Make *notes* in answer to similar points about something you are interested in (foot diseases of earwigs?!).
3   Try telling someone about ONE or OTHER of these – perhaps the class would take an interest?
If anyone asks you a question, remember what it is so that you can include that point any other time you talk on this subject.
4   What sort of impression do you get if someone is full of grumbles, or keeps saying that 'it's boring'?

19.3   Word match

**Head your work
19.3   Word match:
Phrases about
interests**

What do these phrases mean?
1   to take an interest in
2   to have an obsession
3   to do yourself justice
4   to be objective about
5   to do credit to
6   to be involved with
7   to represent
8   to excel at
9   to be distinguished
10   to be noted for

19.4　Interview the interviewer

Job interview or visitor. *They* will ask *you* questions. And when you answer their questions, try to give an answer that can lead on to another question.

**Head your work
19.4　Asking
questions**

1　Which visitor will find out most about the school?
2　Which visitor will have the best impression of the school?
3　Make a list of questions you could ask:
a) a visitor to the school,
b) at an interview.

A few possible questions are given below – and some impossible ones. Choose the suitable ones, and then see how many more you can think of:

a) Why did you decide to visit our school?
Have you visited many other schools?
What sort of accent have you got?
Why aren't you at work just now?
Are there some things you would specially like to hear about?
b) What are the rates of pay?
What are the holiday arrangements?
Will I be Managing Director in the end?
Do you serve second helpings at dinner time?
Can I work with my mates?

19.5 Industrial tests

Many firms set you a test before they take you on.
These tests often include questions on arithmetic, spelling, and general knowledge.
Often the tests also include some questions of a different sort. They may be like these here. Many pupils find they can do better on these questions than on the ones that test their work in class.

Head your work
19.5   Answers to
a test without words

Here are some shapes. You must decide which one of the shapes with a letter above them belong with the three on the left:

1.
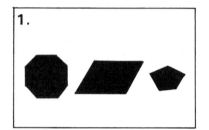

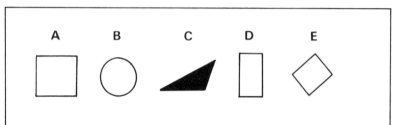

2.
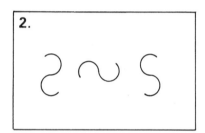

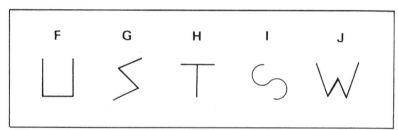

In this test, there is a pair of shapes that are related to each other in some way. You are then given the first one of the next pair. Find the other one, that is related to it in the same way:

3.
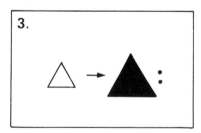

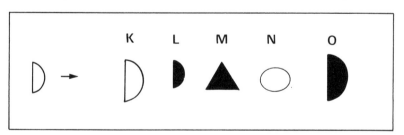

4.
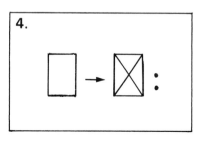

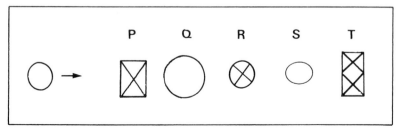

In this test, you are given three pieces. Which ones of the shapes below can be made with these three pieces, following these rules:

each piece can be used only once
the shaded area must be completely covered
one piece must not overlap another piece
you may turn pieces 'over' or 'round'

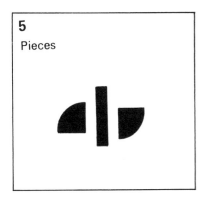

5

Pieces

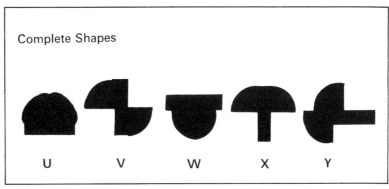

Complete Shapes

U   V   W   X   Y

19.6   Write away!

**Head your work
19.6   Write away!
(and the title)**

**Head your work
19.7   Controversy
about interviews**

1   **I'll tell you what.** All about your school, or your team, or your home town — perhaps you'd prefer to make it a letter to a friend or cousin who has never seen it? Think of the points about it that make it interesting and arrange them in some order.

2   **This is my life.** Tell the events and interests in your own life that you would like to let someone know about. Some of these may be about your home, where you have lived, about brothers and sisters and people you have met, some may be about holidays, or jobs done, teams played in, happy days and unhappy ones.

3   **My family history.** What I know about my parents and grandparents, uncles and aunts, and relations in earlier generations; where they came from, what they did, what they were like; family memories and heirlooms.

19.7   Controversy

1   Interviews are silly. You should get a job by passing a test.
2   Tests are silly. You should be allowed a trial period in a job and they should take you on after that.
3   School teaches us the wrong things the wrong way — we would do much better if school were about . . .
4   My interests are nothing to do with my job and there's no point talking about them.
5   We're often going to be unemployed. But there are so many interesting things to do that we won't get bored.

19.8　Read all about it!

A biography is a book about a person's life. There is always a special appeal to a story written about someone when it is a true story. Many of these people had to face great difficulties at times, and it can be very exciting to see how they dealt with them.

Biographies have been written about explorers, politicians, authors, musicians, sportsmen; and scientists. One important scientist was Louis Pasteur. Some of your class might have died already if it had not been for work done by Pasteur in fighting many different diseases. Every time you have an innoculation, every time a wound is healed, almost every time you eat, your body is feeling the good effects of Pasteur's work. Before Pasteur's time, some of your class would have been likely to die before the age of 15 from diseases you now hardly know — cholera, smallpox, tetanus, rabies, or simply food poisoning. But Pasteur did not find it easy to make people believe there were any germs in the world, because they could not see them.

Head your work
19.8　The life of ＿＿＿

See if you can find out about the life of someone you admire a lot, and write an account of it as a short biography.

Riddle

Why didn't the brilliant young footballer want to be a star?

He thought he'd only come out at night.

19.9 Crossword number nineteen

Clues across

* 1 Things to do with industry (10).
* 6 A word for choosing between this one and that one (2).
  7 Short for 'Automobile Association' (2).
  8 Colour of earth or tree trunks (5).
  11 Short for 'television' (2).
  13 First half of the word 'halt' makes a short laugh (2).
* 15 The idea or picture you get of something (10).
* 17 The change he gave was ____ little (3).
  19 First half of the word 'vote' (2).
  20 Short for 'State Registered Nurse' (2).
* 21 Whether it rhymes or not it is a special way of saying things (4).
  23 Short word found in 'this' (2).
* 24 Showing interest (10).

Clues down

  2 First half of the word 'normally' means the usual thing (4).
  3 To let something fall (4).
  4 A short word of thanks (2).
  5 Bigger than mice, they are a serious pest (4).
* 8 A piece or part (3).
  9 Short for 'Western Region' (2).
* 10 Not ever (5).
* 12 Go to see (5).
* 13 Perhaps you know how to ride one? (5).
  14 A girl's name (3).
* 16 Not all of them, but not none either (4).
  18 To choose, or pick out (3).
  22 Vowels in the word 'poem' (2).

Words from page 116

døgn is a period of 24 hours, a complete night and day. In English if you make a whole day's journey it is not clear whether it takes 12 hours or 24 hours.

pålegg is anything you can put on bread, sweet or savoury. It has a much wider meaning than the English word 'spread'.

bil! is a word shouted in warning when any vehicle is coming along the road. Our word 'traffic' means more than one vehicle, and we have no other word that would do for one, or more than one, vehicle of any type.

20
Advertisements for jobs

20.1 The petrol pump boy

Gary has just got a job on the pumps. It suits him well. He wanted to work with cars and there weren't any jobs he could get on the repairing side. The pay's not bad, either.

He loves those first months. Everyone is friendly. 'Me? Change jobs? Never!'

On November 19th he has his birthday. The boss sees the date on his insurance card. 'What, 17 already Gary? You're growing up too fast, my lad. Suppose you'll be expecting a rise? Comes expensive it does, all for selling a few gallons of petrol.'

He usually gets to work dead on time to open up at 8.0 a.m. He gets on nicely with most of the customers. Sometimes he even gets tips.

November 19th comes round again. 'What, 18 now? Another rise, Gary? Have I got to pay all that just to have the pumps working? I'd rather go self-service.'

Next morning he is ten minutes late (after all, it is the morning after his birthday).

'Where the hell have you been? Get a move on! I'm not having skiving round here! Do you hear?'

Every time a car pulls in all day long, the boss shouts crossly — 'Aren't you there yet, Gary? What the blazes are you playing at?'

When no cars can be seen, it is —

'Come here Gary. Get this cupboard cleaned out. Get those windows polished. Why haven't you done it before?'

Gary gets flustered. He gives a customer the wrong change — 50p too little. The boss hears the customer point it out. He doesn't say anything, but his eyes say plenty. For the rest of the day the boss stands over the till, and watches every penny. He doesn't let Gary knock off until the money in the till has been counted twice — 'Just want to make sure it's all here.'

And it goes on like that. The boss is always in a bad mood. Always sour, always shouting, never trusting him an inch. After a few weeks, Gary gets fed up. He finds another job.

Chris calls in at the garage a few days later. He'd left school in the summer, and hasn't got a job yet. His birthday was in July, so he hasn't been 16 long. The boss takes him on.

'O.K. Chris, that's your lot for today,' says the boss cheerfully. 'You've done a good job for your first day. Off you go home now.'

Head your work
20.1 The petrol pump boy

The story of the petrol pump boy is a true one. It is also a common one.

1 What future had Chris got with this firm?
2 Why did Gary notice a sudden change in the way the boss spoke to him one day?
3 Had Gary ever done anything to deserve the sack?
4 What can happen if someone is sacked without a good reason?
5 What does 'redundancy' mean?
6 What controls are there on employers that make it difficult for them to get rid of staff through redundancy?
7 How does this boss get rid of Gary without upsetting the Unions or breaking the law in any way?
8 Could the same thing happen to you?

20.2 Who are you? Know yourself

Some people like being in charge.
Some like making decisions.
Some like to be told what to do.
Some like to settle.
Some like to move around.

It's a good thing people are different. There's nothing wrong with not wanting to take charge. There's nothing wrong with moving around, or with settling down. It takes all types to make a world.

**Head your work
20.2   Discovering
myself**

But know yourself. And try to find the work to suit yourself.

What sort of answers do you give to these questions? Set out the table carefully for future reference.

Question	Never	Sometimes	Always	Suggest one job of this type
Would you like to work out of doors?				
Would you like to live away from home?				
Would you like to have a job that involves day time travelling?				
Would you like to do some written work?				
Would you like to do some typing?				
Would you like to use your hands?				
Would you like to have to look tidy at work?				
Would you like to work among others of your own age?				
Would you like to meet a lot of other people?				
Would you like to be told what to do each day?				
Would you like to be a foreman or your own boss one day?				
Would you mind a lot if the job finished after a year or two?				
Do you want to be trained as a skilled worker?				

20.3   Word match

**Head your work
20.3   Word match
about jobs**

What is meant by these words when they are used in job advertisements?

applicant
manager
permanent
qualifications
competent

proficient
location
confidence
experience
clerical

142

20.4 Where will you find a job?

Is everyone dying for a chance to pay you £20 or more a week?
Or are you one of the unlucky ones who will have to *look* for a job?
What jobs have you heard of so far that would interest you, and that you might stand a chance of getting? How did you hear of them:

**Head your work
20.4   Jobs I have
heard about**

1   From the careers teacher? What job? What is it like?
2   From the Youth Employment Officer?
3   From employment agencies?
4   From parents, family, or friends?
5   From the local paper?
6   From any other place?

20.5 What's involved in the job?

**Head your work
19.5   Discovering
the job**

When you see an advertisement for a job that you might be interested in, you need to think whether it would suit you – if you are lucky enough to get it.

Check the job with a questionnaire that follows exactly the same pattern as the one in 19.2
How does the job fit with what you wanted then? If there are big differences, how did they come about? Does the difference mean you have changed your mind – or that you got an answer wrong?

AGRICULTURAL MACHINERY MANUFACTURER, situated in pleasant rural area, is expanding its design and development section and requires

TWO MECHANICAL DRAUGHTSMEN/WOMEN

These are permanent positions with good prospects for persons with drive and enthusiasm. Knowledge of agricultural machinery and production engineering methods an advantage.
Age 25 to 40.

CLERICAL ASSISTANTS
(Clerical Grade 1)

School-Leavers are required to be trained as Administrative Assistants. Preference will be given five or more 'O' level and/or two 'A' level ssful applicants will receive training in all ncil's functions.

SHORTHAND T

Pay according to standards achieved — £40.50 p.w. Proficiency allowa p.w., Class A £4.80 p.w.. Five-da 9½ days public and privilege holi leave allowance of 18 days. Non ation scheme.

Please **telephone** Wallingf

ASSISTANT FOR LARGE OUTDOOR SOW HERD
A fully experienced or college-trained person required. Driving licence essential. A considerable amount of overtime required to be worked. First-class modernised House with garage and garden available on edge of village, close to school and 3 miles from centre of Devizes.
A good basic wage will be offered according to experience and ability.

SECRETARY
required for busy travel office
Position involves dealing with the public at large!

the 5th time

DANT

MMER FITTER

d to help maintain a fleet of **25 AEC / Leyland / Bedford Vehicles.**
llent working conditions, with free overalls and boots
Location: Wallingford

Press Opera

Rates of pay: £35.60 per 40 hours for 20-years-old a Proportionately less for those under 20. Subsidised allowance. Works Coaches from Calne, Netheravon a Pewsey with pick-ups en route. No Saturdays.

Head your work
20.6   Write away!
(and the title)

20.6   Write away!

1   **Me & Co. Ltd.** A big day-dream: how you built up your own business and ran a big concern; what you made, and what you liked about it all.

2   **£50 not enough.** Even if they paid you £50 a week for doing that job, it would not be enough. What's wrong with it, how it compares with other jobs, why is your labour worth so much? (What's the job? Mucking out pigs? In a noisy factory? Coal mining?)

3   **If I go on the dole.** What would life be like on the dole? Is it better than working? Is it boring? Do you feel rotten because no one wants you to work for them? How would you spend your time? Who do you know who is on the dole?

20.7   Controversy

1   I don't care how often I change jobs: I couldn't stick the same job for long.
2   Careers teachers and Y.E.O.'s never bother with people who won't get 5 O-levels.
3   If 16-year-olds can't get jobs it's only because they haven't looked hard enough.
4   The best way to get a job is through the grapevine – when someone knows about a job going and tells you about it.
5   I live in the wrong place to have a decent career. If only I lived in _____ I could _____ .

20.8   Read all about it

The Second World War was not just a war of big battles, but it was also a war of invention and discovery. The people who developed radar systems had a big effect on the result of the war, and so of course did the people who worked on the Atomic Bomb.

The Nazis were also trying to make an Atomic Bomb, and if they had managed it first they would presumably have used it against us. One of the things they needed for their work was something called 'heavy water', which is not easy to come by. In 1940 the Nazis took over Norway, and one of the factories that fell into their control was making heavy water. It was therefore very important to blow up the factory and stop their supply of heavy water.

The small group of men whose job it was to do this made sure that the Nazis lost the race to make the bomb first, and so the whole world has much to thank them for.

The story of how they managed to blow up a factory that the Nazis were guarding very carefully is told in a book called *Assault in Norway* by Thomas Gallagher.

**Head your work
20.8   It was war!**

What event in the war that you have heard about, seen a film about, or read about, has interested you most? Can you write an account of it, explaining what was specially impressive about it?

Riddle

Where did Marty the Martian look for the 'responsible post' that was advertised in the jobs column?

In the Post Office.

20.9 Crossword number twenty

Clues across

* 1   Having a certainty about something (10).

* 9   Here and there, in one place or another (6).

10   First three letters of the word 'woven' (3).

11   Pigs may live in one (3).

12   You hear with them (4).

15   Your ears are on each side of it (4).

*17   Practice, knowledge that comes from doing it (10).

*20   Losing your job because there is no work to do any more (10).

23   A very fast sort of bicycle (5).

*25   Gary gave the wrong change, _____ little (3).

26   Vowels in the word 'carrot' (2).

27   Short for 'Thank-you' (2).

28   Letters before I V V in the alphabet (3).

*29   Good at doing it (10).

*32   Mend something (6).

33   Consonants in the word 'youth' (3).

Clues down

* 1   Jobs or sorts of employment (7).

2   A word for choosing between this one and that one (2).

3   The opposite of yes (2).

4   Disturbance, or too much attention to something (4).

5   One after another, arranged in a fair way (2, 4).

6   The letters before E E Z in the alphabet (3).

7   Short for 'Company' (2).

8   To get out of, avoid (5).

10   A name that sounds like a little bird; one man with this name designed St Paul's Cathedral (5).

13   Used to chop things, such as wood (3).

14   Consonants in the word 'rope' (2).

*15   What we do with our ears (4).

*16   A written record, often about money spent (7).

18   The letters before F V B in the alphabet (3).

19   A thought in your head (4).

21   To sag a bit, like a dying flower (5).

*22   The Y.H.A. is short for '_____ Hostel Association' (5).

24   Letters before D U J J in the alphabet (4).

*25   Those people (4).

*26   'We're' and 'They're' stand for 'we' or 'they' _____ (3).

29   Short for 'public relations' (2).

30   Short for 'Football Association' (2).

31   Short for 'Cash Register' (2).

21
Spelling
trick words

There are different ways of remembering things.
- Sometimes we talk of a 'photographic memory' – you seem to be able to remember something just like a photograph.
- Sometimes one can remember by working out the answer, using rules like: i before e except straight after c – Remember?
- Sometimes one can remember by 'hearing it again' inside your head.
- Sometimes you need a trick to remember it by, because it won't come right any other way.

It's specially those *confusing* things that are very much alike, that need tricks.

Like how many days there are in each month.
Or some common words in spelling that keep getting mixed up.

A trick to remember something by is called a mnemonic (said NEE-MON-IC).
Mnemonics often don't make much sense. They may work best if they are specially silly. They are just meant to help you remember something.

Head your work
21.1 Mnemonics for general knowledge

1   How does the mnemonic 'nobody eats Shredded Wheat' help you remember the points of the compass?
2   How many days are there in each month of the year? Can you discover the mnemonic that helps you remember them?

21.2 Some tricky words to spell

● Have you ever got mixed up between those two words 'know' and 'no'?
Try this mnemonic:

> If you **know** it, it is in your head. And your head has got ears. You hear with your ears but you can't hear the ears themselves. And the word 'know' has got two letters you can't hear, like ears, one on each side.

> But **No** has got nothing, no clothes on;
> it means nothingness, and no, it's got nothing.

● Have you ever got mixed up between those two words 'hear' and 'here'?
Which sort do you need your ears for?
You h**ear** with your **ears**. Use the same letters.
And you keep those letters when you have h**ear**d it also.

● What about 'where' and 'wear'?
Well, do you w**ear** clothes on your **ear**? At least you wear them near the ear.
And if you don't know w**here** it is, when you find it, won't you say, 'It's **here**!'?

● Have you ever got mixed up between those three words:
there
their
they're

Try this mnemonic —

Are you looking for your money
HERE   or   t**HERE?**

There often (though not always) means the other place from **here** and it is spelt the same with a 't' on the front.

Their money belongs to them, and so each of them will say '**I** want some of it because it's mine.' If it belongs to someone, it will have an I in it, because someone will say 'I want it'. **'The belonging their belongs to I.'**

They're means 'they are'. You need to use your computer memory on this one. Work it out. If you could put in the two words 'they are', and it still makes sense, then use 'they're' with the ' (apostrophe).

● Have you ever got mixed up between 'whole' and 'hole'?
Didn't the mouse make a **hole** in a **whole** piece of cheese?
Isn't there a **HOLE** in w**HOLE**?

Head your work
21.2 Using spelling
mnemonics

● Have you ever got mixed up between the two words 'who' and 'how'?
They have the same letters in a different order.
Who is what the owl asks: 'Who are you? Too-wit, too-woo'. (Begins with *w*.)
How is what you ask a cow: 'How now, brown cow?' (Ends with -ow).

● Have you ever got mixed up between the three words:
too
two
to

It's too much! Too difficult! Too many rules! Too many mnemonics! Too many letters! **'Too' meaning too much has too many o's.**
Numbers can't count! Two tries to be three – three letters. **Two – the number that tries to beat itself. To – the little word, modest and quiet;** often said very quickly (I'm going t' work), and written quickly also: to.

Now these words won't trick you any more. So you can fill in all the right spellings in these sentences. Use only the words from these mnemonics.
1 It was _____ much trouble _____ make _____ copies of the picture.
2 What are those boys doing? _____ looking for _____ ball over _____ .
3 I want to know his name but I don't know _____ to spell _____ he is.
4 I can't _____ the music properly _____ .
5 _____ did I put the clothes I'm going to _____ ?
6 _____ Miss, I don't _____ where it is.
7 The _____ pitch was covered in _____ made by the voles.

21.3 Word match

Head your work
21.3 Word match
on similar looking
words

There are some confusing pairs of words. Look up the differences in meanings between the words in these pairs and put them down.
1 affect – effect
2 breath – breathe
3 practice – practise
4 complementary – complimentary
5 personal – personnel

Head your work
21.4　One letter
makes a muddle

21.4　One letter makes all the difference

Sometimes there are two words that look (and perhaps sound) very much the same, but one letter makes all the difference. Use a dictionary if necessary, and explain these sentences. In your answer, put down *both* the confusing words and show you know the difference between them.

1　The station master went to buy his morning paper. When he saw the notice outside the shop he waved his green flag and blew his whistle.

2　John couldn't spell as well as Jane, so he brought a wheel chair as soon as he had the letter from Jane saying 'We are going to move farther into the country.'

3　The mayor thought that a big gun was coming when he heard that the canon would visit the town's church.

21.5   Just what did he say?

Right back on page 22 we mentioned speech marks.
Speech marks were used round the words someone actually said.
But what did he say?

The judge said that the witness said that the accused's mother had said to the accused's father that he had said that if he had said what he said he had said he would do what he had said he would do if he said it again and thrash him.
— Excuse me, milud, who would thrash who? And what had he said?

The important thing is that speech marks are only used round the exact words that someone said; they are not used if you 'borrow' the words to make your own report.

'Direct' speech
'If you say that again I'll thrash you,' said Dad.

'Reported' speech
Dad said that if I said that again he would thrash me.

**Head your work
21.5   Reported speech**

1   Which words that Dad used have been changed in the reported speech?
2   Which one word has been added in the reported speech? Why is this word very important?
3   Can you answer the lawyer's question at the end of the court passage above?
4   Try writing out one of these passages as a series of short sentences, with direct speech:

Jane asked Sally if she had ever ridden a pony. Sally said she had, because her cousin Elizabeth had one of her own. Jane wanted to know what the pony was like, and Sally said that it was a dapple grey, and had a very sweet nature.

Mark asked Brian if he had ever camped out. Brian said he had on a Scout camp once, when they had done a three-day hike. Mark wanted to know if Brian had a tent of his own, but Brian said they had used the Scout tents, which were big bell tents.

21.6 Write away!

Head your work
21.6   Write away!
(and the title)

1   **And then she said.** Can you make up a short story in which there are two chatter-boxes that keep on talking and talking? You would probably do best to put most of it down in direct speech.

2   **Act one, scene one. Take!** Can you write a script for a play or a television programme? Choose any subject you like from a murder story to an adventure trip.

3   **Hello. Been here long?** Pretend you have a long time to spend *either* on the riverbank fishing *or* in a cafeteria in town. Put down the conversation you might have with other people who might come and join you for a bit.

21.7 Controversy

Head your work
21.7   Controversy
about public issues

1   Speed limits on British roads are too low.
2   Concorde was a waste of money. The Government should build buses instead.
3   School meals cost too much.
4   Nationalizing industries will never pay.
5   Does it matter whether you smoke or not? You can choose low-tar fags anyway.

21.8 Read all about it

Head your work
21.8   (and choose
a title)

Poems are often protests about things, and they get their strength from the poet's forthright, personal way of saying it. How many poems of this type have you read?

Study a few poems of this sort, and see how they are built to have 'punch-lines' that make their points strongly, and then try your hand at a poem of this sort yourself.

Riddle
Why can time see when thyme can't?

Because it's got an i. (eye)

21.9 Crossword number twenty-one

Clues across

1 People in your family are ____ to you (7).

* 6 Your earnings (3).

7 A short word you can always use instead of your name (1).

* 8 The elected head of a Town Council (5).

*11 It helps to remember the compass if nobody does this to Shredded Wheat (4).

*12 Did you write most ____ your story in direct speech? (2).

*13 What does the producer shout after saying 'Act one, Scene One'? (4).

15 This word, for the group of people who meet to decide what the company is to do, makes them sound as if they are made of wood (5).

17 Second and third letters of the word 'never' (2).

18 A short steep slope for cars to go up (4).

21 A short word of surprise (2).

22 Short for 'Air Training Corps' (3).

*23 It won't happen – not ever (5).

25 Answers that you make hoping that you will be right by luck – not because you know they are right (7).

Clues down

* 1 A mnemonic is to help you do this (11).

* 2 These little marks are used when letters are left out of a word like 'they're' (11).

* 3 Sticky substance in cigarettes that harms your lungs (3).

4 Last two letters of the words 'they', 'grey', and 'obey' (2).

* 5 These are important points between words like 'breath' and 'breathe' or 'cloths' and 'clothes' (11).

9 Short for 'Automobile Association' (2).

10 An advertiser might write it this funny way if he wanted to ask you 'why tea?' rather than coffee? (2).

12 People often say the names of these two letters when they mean that something is all right (2).

14 Short for 'advertisement' (2).

16 You may have used this word in Science lessons for eggs, such as the eggs of fish. It looks a bit like 'oval' (3).

*19 Sometimes people like to change from one house to another farther into the country (4).

*20 What you hear with (4).

23 Letters before 'O' and 'H' (2).

24 Two letters that stand for 'Europe' that some people put on cars (2).

22
Writing letters of application

22.1 Act out

Writing off for a job?

If not now, perhaps you will some time in the next year or two.

When you do, your letter speaks for you. Your letter has got to be good enough that they will ask you to come for interview. Little things in the letter can matter a lot when there's nothing else to go by.

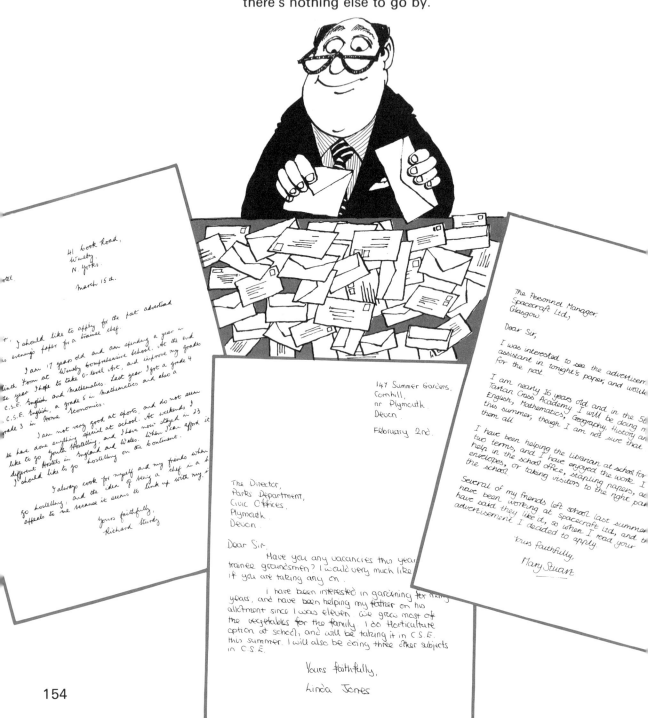

41 Gook Road,
Wimbley,
N. Yorks.

march 15th.

... I should like to apply for the post advertised in this evening's paper for a trainee chef.

I am 17 years old and am spending a year in the sixth form at Wimbley comprehensive school. At the end of the year I hope to take O-level Arc, and improve my grades in C.S.E. English and Mathematics. Last year I got a grade 4 in C.S.E. English, a grade 5 in Mathematics and also a grade 3 in Home Economics.

I am not very good at sports, and do not seem to have done anything special at school. At weekends I like to go youth Hostelling, and I have now stayed in 23 different Hostels in England and Wales. When I can afford it I should like to go hostelling on the Continent.

I always cook for myself and my friends when I go hostelling, and the idea of being a chef in a hostel appeals to me because it seems to link up with my ...

Yours faithfully,
Richard Sturdy

---

147 Summer Gardens,
Cornhill,
nr Plymouth
Devon

February 2nd.

The Director,
Parks Department,
Civic Offices,
Plymouth,
Devon.

Dear Sir,

Have you any vacancies this year for trainee groundsmen? I would very much like ... if you are taking any on.

I have been interested in gardening for many years, and have been helping my father on his allotment since I was eleven. We grow most of the vegetables for the family. I do Horticulture option at school, and will be taking it in C.S.E. this summer. I will also be doing three other subjects in C.S.E.

Yours faithfully,

Linda Jones

The Personnel Manager,
Spacecraft Ltd,
Glasgow.

Dear Sir,

I was interested to see the advertisement assistant in tonight's paper, and would ... for the post.

I am nearly 16 years old and in the 5th Tartan Cross Academy. I will be doing ... English, Mathematics, Geography, History an... this summer, though I am not sure that ... them all.

I have been helping the librarian at school for two terms, and I have enjoyed the work. I... help in the school office, stapling papers, ac... envelopes, or taking visitors to the right part the school.

Several of my friends left school last summer ... have been working at Spacecraft Ltd, and th... have said they like it, so when I read your advertisement I decided to apply.

Yours faithfully,

Mary Stuart

Divide into groups of four or five.

1   Pretend you are the bosses. You are going to choose a new employee for your firm. Decide what sort of job it is and what the person will have to do.

2   When you have done this, you must make an advertisement for the rest of the class (see chapter 20).

3   Everyone in the class must write letters of application for the jobs advertised by the different groups. If possible, write for two or three different jobs. Use false names.

4   Next, each 'Board of Directors' sorts the applications for your advertisement to decide which applicant you want to interview − also, choose a 'reserve' candidate.

5   Last of all, interview your chosen applicant, and, if necessary, the reserve candidate (see 22.5 about interviews).

22.2   How did you make your choice?

Head your work
22.2   How we chose
our candidate

1   What made you choose your 'best' candidate? His or her:
age
qualifications
handwriting
address
interests
or something else

2   What made you reject some of the candidates? Their:
handwriting
spelling mistakes
envelopes
short letters
something they said wrong in the letter
or something else

3   Make some suggestions about the things an employer would be looking for when he reads a letter of application, and how he would choose his short-list.

4   Was one candidate better than the others in the interview? If so, what made the difference? If not, how could you choose between the candidates?

22.3   Word match

What do these people do? Find out as much as you can about their trades. A dictionary can help you a bit. Perhaps you can find out more in a careers library?

skipper   steeplejack
architect   chauffeur
joiner   compositor
plumber   draper
auditor   accountant

22.4   The framework of a letter

If you are asked to write a letter of application, you don't need to write a book; but you mustn't send just a note.

Try writing the best honest letter about yourself that you can manage, using these points as a framework. Be careful to set the letter out carefully, to make a draft, check it, and choose the right ways of saying things.

1   Be careful with laying out your address, the date, the 'Dear Sir,' and a heading: 'Application for _____ '.
2   A short bit to begin — what you are applying for, and how you know about the vacancy.
3   The most important points about yourself — age, school, examinations you plan to take, *or* when you are planning to leave school.
4   Other important points about yourself — skills, hobbies, part-time jobs, interests, or a good reputation.
5   Why you are specially interested in the job you are applying for — best of all, something that follows from numbers 3 and 4 above.
6   Your signature.

22.5   Making the most of the interview

If you have written a good letter you will have given your interviewer some things he can ask you about.

Before you go to the interview, put your mind onto these points so you can tell him more about them.

'So you like woodwork then. What have you made?' Explain what you have done, what equipment you have used, what types of wood you had, and what happened to the furniture, models, or boats afterwards.

'So you go baby sitting do you? Do you like it?' Explain how often you go; how old the 'babies' are (ten year old cousins perhaps?). Have one or two stories ready to tell — best of all, ones that show how well you managed when they were sick, or yelled for their parents.

Choose *at least three*, and as many as possible, of the 'interviewer's questions' from the list below, and write answers – as real as possible – along the lines of the two examples above. You may change the word underlined to another word to suit your special interests.

1   So you play hockey? Do you like the game?
2   You go fishing a lot? What have you caught?
3   You are good at Maths you say? What can you do?
4   You have heard about this firm before? Why do you want to work for it?
5   You are doing four exams. How are you going to get on in them?
6   You like cooking, I see. How much do you do?
7   You're at the Comprehensive school. Do you like it?
8   You'll be 16 soon. Are you looking forward to it?
9   You've been working in a shop. How have you got on?
10   So you know Mrs Smith? How do you get on with her?

22.6 Write away

Head your work
22.6 Write away!
(and the title)

1   **The people I work for.** Saturday job, odd jobs, paper round, baby minding – anyone who pays you. What they are like, what they expect you to do, how they ask you to do things. Did you have an interview when you got the job? If so, what did they ask?

2   **Double my age.** Try to imagine yourself as you will be when you are around 30 years old. What do you think you will be like then? What jobs might you have had? Where will you be living? Try to be realistic in thinking what the future might have in store for you with just a little bit of luck.

3   **We're all different.** Think of a lot of different sorts of jobs. Say what you can about the work there is to be done in each job, and then describe the sort of person you think would be good at doing each of these. If you like you can include bus conductor, milkman, teacher, architect, secretary, receptionist, doctor, fireman, policeman, steeplejack, nurse and cowherd.

22.7 Controversy

Head your work
22.7 Controversy
about work

1 There's no point putting my hobbies down in a letter. They've nothing to do with the job I'd go for.
2 People who have jobs work too long and earn too much. It would be much better to have twice as many jobs for half the time each.
3 What is life for? Is death the end of it all? Where does work fit into your thinking about life?
4 I've been at school for 11 years. I don't want to be in training for another 3 or 4 years.
5 People care more for their machines than for other people these days.

22.8 Read all about it!

Fishing is probably one of the most popular hobbies. Many is the story that has been written about it — and especially about the 'one that got away'.

Sometimes fishing is not just a hobby — it's a job; a tough job, which needs courage and strength and on which your livelihood depends. Hemingway's story *The Old Man and the Sea* is a brilliant story of one man and one fish — it is worth reading every word.

Head your work
22.8 Got it!

Have you got a fishing story to tell? Even if you have never touched a rod in your life, you must have seen thousands of fishermen sitting glumly at work. Real or imaginary, try your hand at a good yarn.

Riddle
What is the worst thing about tea-break?

The end of it.

22.9 Crossword number twenty-two

Clues across

2 A place where you can spend the night, which is not as big as a hotel (3).

4 In hot weather it is nice to have drinks cooled this way (4).

* 6 Places where you go to learn (7).

9 First three letters of the word 'along' (3).

10 Last two letters of the word 'thud' (2).

12 Consonants in the word 'house' (2).

*14 You take one to show how much you know (11).

17 If you write 'time' backwards you make a word that means to 'send out' (light or radio waves) (4).

18 Planes that fly across the Atlantic are _____ -Atlantic airliners (5).

19 The subject that is to do with finding out about life or machines or chemicals (7).

21 A long and difficult journey (there are stories on television about making these journeys among the stars) (4).

22 Colour of a traffic light to stop you (3).

Clues down

1 Met or come across, perhaps by chance (11).

2 Letters after H H G in the alphabet (3).

3 They are the letters before O F P in the alphabet (3).

5 Consonants in the word 'deal' (2).

6 A cross person does this to a door (5).

7 A sort of paper with rows of pictures and a few words on each picture. Boys and girls like to read it (5).

8 What your shoes will do if you polish them enough (5).

9 Used for chopping wood (3).

11 Socks that have been mended (6).

13 The signal sent from a ship in distress (3).

15 For a lady, the word is 'she', for a man the word is 'he', and for a thing the word is _____ (2).

16 Stick together quickly (4).

20 Short word in the middle of 'splitting' (2).

23
Famous names

If you've read the bit above you've heard of them now.
Which ones had you heard of before?
And why should you have heard of them all?
Who cares?
And why?
And are there others you should have heard of?

**Head your work
23.1   Things I have
heard of**

1   Which of these things do you expect every other
British person of your age to have heard about — so that
you can talk about them without special explanation (look
up any that you are not sure of)?
a) aeroplanes   acrobatics   acoustics   atlases   apertures?
b) singing   shillelaghs   Smithfield Market   socialism   sex
2   Which television stars would you expect people to have
heard of?
3   Which politicians do people expect you to have heard of?
4   Which explorers have you heard of, and where did
they go?
5   Which inventors have you heard of, and what did they
work on?

23.2   A world without stories

Television scripts.
Film scripts.
News bulletins.
Press reports.
Magazines and books.
Plays and poems.

There are stories wherever you turn, stories you come across every day.

But it wasn't always so.

Can you imagine a time when people had never seen a play, or read anything at all, not to mention having no radio or television?

And yet the people who built the oldest buildings we are still using in this country never enjoyed any of these things.

So the authors who invented these or made new sorts of entertainment were not just important in their own day: they have given you your entertainment also. What is more, what they wrote is usually still worth reading or watching. Use the library to check the answers to this quiz. Which team is the winner here? Right or wrong?

Around Britain Quiz

3   Which of these authors wrote some of the first novels?
Daniel Defoe, Charles Dickens, Emily Bronte, Ian Fleming

Know-alls: Charles Dickens.

4   Which of these authors wrote a very long poem called
'The Rime of the Ancient Mariner'?
Fielding, Kipling, Milton, Thomson, Coleridge

The Wise: Thomson.

5   Which of these authors was one of the first to write
good science fiction?
H. G. Wells, Sir Walter Scott, Agatha Christie, John Buchan

Know-alls: H. G. Wells.

6   Which of these authors is a Russian whose stories tell
us what life is like inside the Communist world?
Steinbeck, Solzenhitzen, Ibsen, Chekhov

The Wise: Solzenhitzen.

7   Which of these authors was an American?
Sir Winston Churchill, Sir Bertrand Russell, Robert Frost,
John Wyndham

Know-alls: Sir Winston Churchill.

8   Who invented the 'James Bond' series?
T. S. Eliot, Ian Fleming, D. H. Lawrence, Thomas Hardy

The Wise: Ian Fleming.

Try to make up your own quiz for your class along these lines. You could look up authors from the list below and collect information about them to use in your questions.

Hans Christian Andersen   Jane Austen   Stan Barstow
Mrs Beeton   William Blake   Enid Blyton   Ray Bradbury
Geoffrey Chaucer   Agatha Christie   Arthur C. Clarke
Sir Arthur Conan Doyle   Gerald Durrell   C. S. Forester
Paul Gallico   Alan Garner   Ernest Hemingway   Homer
Fred Hoyle   Henry James   James Joyce   Edward Lear
C. S. Lewis   Hugh Lofting   Alistair MacLean   A. A. Milne
John Milton   Ogden Nash   George Orwell   Samuel Pepys
William Shakespeare   G. B. Shaw   Nevil Shute   Jonathan
Swift   J. R. R. Tolkein   Mark Twain   Jules Verne
William Wordsworth   W. B. Yeats

23.3   Word match

What is the difference between:
a report and a bulletin
a script and a play
verse and prose
a pioneer and an inventor
drama and mime

23.4   The pioneers

Geoffrey Chaucer was almost the first person to write anything in the language we now call English. His most famous work was the 'Canterbury Tales', a collection of stories told to each other by a group of people on a journey to Canterbury. When four of these tales were made into a play in London recently it was a hit show that ran for many years.

William Shakespeare was in the first group of playwrights to make any plays like we see nowadays in the theatre. He was one of the first theatre managers. Many of the plays he wrote were among the finest that have ever been written in any language. He is famous all over the world, and his plays are always running in many places.

Daniel Defoe wrote a book called 'Robinson Crusoe', which started off a whole set of stories about imaginary adventures and survival.

Jonathan Swift wrote 'Gulliver's Travels' not as a children's book, but as a comment on how people behave. The children's story cuts out Gulliver's visit to Laputa and the Houyhnhnms and also cuts out a lot about Lilliput and Brobdingnag. Swift was an important writer who had a big effect on what the government did, particularly about bad government in Ireland.

The Globe Theatre

Jane Austen (above)
George Orwell (below)

Jane Austen was one of the first of the lady novelists. Her books, as well as those of the Bronte sisters and the later George Eliot (a lady) are still very popular indeed.

Robert Burns was a Scottish poet, who wrote a lot of popular poems in his own dialect.

William Wordsworth was a poet who tried very hard to make his poems simple, and to use largely everyday words. He liked to write about country people and country places, and his poetry started off a lot of other poets on the same lines.

Charles Dickens was a novelist who wrote stories that came out as serials and were enormously popular in his own day. They have been read a lot ever since.

H. G. Wells wrote some of the first science-fiction stories, for example when he imagined Martians arriving in England in his book 'The War of the Worlds'.

1   What are the nine things that were pioneered by these nine authors?
2   Put down the titles of a few books, plays or poems that you have read that might fit into *one* of these types, and say who the pioneer of this type was.
3   Try to find a copy of at least one book, play, or poem by each of these authors, and have a look at it. Make a note of which one you have looked at and what you have found out about it.

23.5   Some modern names

D. H. Lawrence was an English novelist who wrote a lot of very good novels, especially about the people who lived in the mining villages of the Midlands.

W. B. Yeats was an Irish poet who had a great effect on his countrymen at the time when the Republic of Ireland became independent from Britain. Some of his poems and plays built up a national pride and influenced the people in the way they fought for, and used, their independence.

Dylan Thomas was a Welsh poet who is specially remembered for capturing the sound and spirit of a Welsh village in his play 'Under Milk Wood'.

J. R. R. Tolkien was a writer who wrote stories based on imaginary animals (Hobbits, dwarves and others), and encouraged a great vogue of such stories, and enthusiastic followers of his imaginary world.

George Orwell has had a great influence on our thinking about communism and the controls the state imposes; particularly in his novel '1984', but also in his book

'Animal Farm', which, in its full text, is a comment on the Russian Revolution, and not the children's story it is sometimes taken to be.

**Head your work
23.5 Famous modern authors**

1   Which one of these authors wrote 'Lady Chatterley's Lover', and why is it famous?
2   Which of these authors wrote about Llaregyb Hill?
3   Which of these authors wrote 'The Lord of the Rings'?
4   Which of these authors wrote a poem called 'Easter 1916'?
5   Which of these authors wrote about Big Brother, and who was Big Brother?

23.6   Write away!

**Head your work
23.6   Write away!
(and the title)**

1   **No radio, books or plays.** How do you imagine people would spend their free time without modern entertainment?

2   **The best film I ever saw** (or play). Where was it, what was it, what happened in it, and what did you like about it?

3   **Poems I like.** What sort of poetry do you like? Which are your favourite poems, or the best bits of them? Collect together some special bits and say what you like about them.

23.7   Controversy

**Head your work
23.7   Controversy
about entertainment**

1   The serial plays on the box are the only ones worth watching.
2   Theatres are only for posh people.
3   I don't believe anyone cares if you've heard of Shakespeare or not.
4   Books can't really alter how people think or behave.
5   There's no point bothering with the past: there's enough to do now.

23.8   Read all about it!

What sort of creatures do you imagine when you think of invaders from Outer Space? Daleks? Small people from flying saucers? Robots? Giants?
If you have not read H G Wells' *War of the Worlds*, or seen the film of the book, you may not have thought of such weak creatures in such dangerous machines as he imagined.

**Head your work
23.8   Invaders from outer space**

Try your own hand at a story of an invasion from outer space. Where would the attack come? Or would it be just a visit? Perhaps you were the one who saw it all begin?

23.9 Crossword number twenty-three

Clues across

* 1 He wrote the 'Canterbury Tales' nearly 600 years ago (7).
5 The other way from down (2).
6 Change the 'v' to a 'd' in 'above' and you have another word for a house (5).
10 Short for 'Readers' Union' or 'Rugby Union' (2).
11 Short for 'Further Education' (2).
12 The letters before G X in the alphabet (2).
13 Short for the 'Royal Air Force' (3).
14 A god of the ancient Egyptians, whose name looks like the first half of the word 'race' (2).
15 What the audience shouts if they are very pleased with the performance and they want to see or hear it again (6).
17 A boy's name that rhymes with 'even' (6).

Clues down

* 1 An author who writes many stories of science fiction (6).
2 One of Shakespeare's plays was called 'Much _____ about Nothing' (3).
3 An actor begins to speak when he hears this (3).
4 First half of the word 'epic' (2).
* 7 Famous poet from Scotland (5).
* 8 One of the first novelists (5).
* 9 He wrote *Tom Sawyer*, *Huckleberry Finn*, and the *Life on the Mississippi* among other things (5).
11 Fiction is about stories. What is non-fiction about? (4).
12 This word means you don't have to pay for it (4).
16 The letters before S W in the alphabet (2).

24
Conclusion

24.1 You should have heard what Dad said!

School leavers better qualified

says Headmistress

Miss S. Shaw, Headmistress of Seaton Comprehensive School, said today that the pupils leaving her school at the end of term were 'better qualified to work and live in the modern world' than ever before.

Head your work
24.1 The Seaton Star report

1 Did Miss Shaw say anything about passing examinations?
Do you think exams are an important part of being 'qualified', or is your general knowledge more important than exam grades?
2 Do you *feel* qualified to 'work and live in the modern world' as Miss Shaw said? If not, in what ways do you not feel properly qualified?
3 Do you think you have learnt everything you will need to know for working and making a living in the modern world?
4 Have you gained the basic knowledge and experience that will help you go on learning when you leave school, if you want to? – learning on the job, at college, on courses, and at home? (Check list overleaf.)

Can you read and write?
Can you make notes?
Can you spell fairly well now?
Can you use a library?
Can you discuss things with people?
What other basic knowledge and experience have you got that might be useful?

24.2 Learning things we do not experience

We often have to learn about things we cannot see.

'In the car factories in Detroit the way they do this is . . .'
'In Ghana, where these cocoa beans grow, they pick them when . . .'
'In Tokyo, where these parts are made, the temperatures . . .'

When we hear sentences like this we use knowledge we have got to help us imagine the things we have never seen. Then we can understand the point that is being explained to us.

Head your work
24.2   Knowing things
I have not seen

1   What does 'Detroit' bring to your mind?
American accent
Skyscrapers
A map of the U.S.A.
Railway lines
Or something else — what?

2   Why does 'Detroit' mean something to you?
From films
From lessons in school
From photographs
From something outside school – what?

3   What does 'Ghana' bring to your mind?
Black faces
Hot weather
A map of Africa
Cocoa forests
Or something else – what?

4   Why does 'Ghana' mean something to you?

5   What does 'Tokyo' bring to your mind?
Yellow faces
A huge city
A map of Asia
The Olympic Games

6   Why does 'Tokyo' mean something to you?

Do you think that Dad who was discussing the Seaton Star had missed the point?

Perhaps the school he went to ages ago was a bad one. Lots of them were. Many teachers were away in the War. All sorts of people helped in school. Classes were big and the pupils were often badly taught. But that was in Dad's day.

A school doesn't try to teach you everything you need to know. How can it? It tries to give you the chance to learn what you need to know later.

In a year or two you could each come back and teach your teachers something:
about metal fatigue
about food processing
about deep-sea fishing
about modern agriculture
about computer systems
about conveyor-belt work
– or what else would you like to mention?

7   In each case what you had learnt would have built on things you had done in school. What 'groundwork' would have been done in school for each of these areas of specialist knowledge that you had gained outside school?

8   The groundwork itself is built on the most important area of knowledge of all. Which of these is it?

books	maths	science	P.E.
handwriting	drawing	words	spelling

24.3   **Word match**

How much Science do you know? Can you explain these terms? If not, use a dictionary to help you. Think of each word in the scientific sense.

gravity   capacity   density   resonance   reflection

24.4   **It all begins as a baby**

Head your work
24.4   It all begins
as a baby

1   Why doesn't Detroit or Ghana or Tokyo mean anything to a small child who has just learnt to talk?

2   If you explain that these are the names of places, would you expect the child to imagine:

a)   a place like the one in which he lives?

b)   what it is really like abroad?

3   What sort of things does a small child first learn to name? (See page 128.)

4   How many of these things are things that the child can touch, feel, or play with?

5   How many, and which ones, of these words do you think would fit with what a small child knows about a *spoon*? (He or she will not know these words at that age: but how many of the ideas behind the words will he know?)

hard	steel	Mummy	heavy	disinfect
smooth	handle	food	bang	diet
cold	5 ml	shine	falls	temperature

6   What, then, was the ground work for learning about: gravity, capacity, density, resonance, reflection?

24.5   **What did you learn before starting school?**

What a child learns before ever going to school can make a difference to his whole life.

A child learns by exploring, trying, playing, and most of all by talking.

That's why the doll is such a good teacher. So is the teddy bear.

Toy animals and toy dolls allow a child to talk and talk. The toys never get headaches and they never say 'shut up'. Most of them are good at answering (in pretend voices!). There must also be something to talk about. Small children need to go to new places, have new songs to sing and new ideas to talk about. They need to use their fingers as well as their tongues. Building toys like Lego and Meccano, or Play-doh and Plasticine, allow them to make models of things they have seen. Children need the 'Action Replay' to fix the words, ideas, and events in their memories.

1   Find a few nursery rhymes, and think what a child is learning about while he sings these rhymes — particularly if some action or game is used at the same time.

2   What have you ever learnt after hearing or seeing it just *once*, without revising, or talking about it, or writing, or making something, afterwards?

3   Toys never get headaches. Why does this make them such good teachers? Who might not do so well?

4   What ideas can you have without words?

5   Toys never explain or use new words. Why is it so important for children that their parents should use new words and make the meanings clear?

24.6   Write away!

**Head your work
24.6   Write away!
(and the title)**

1   **Toys for children.** What do you think are the best toys for children? If you had £100 to spend on buying toys for two children aged 3½ and 1, what would you buy for them, and why would you choose these things? (Pretend they have clothes and food, but no toys or books yet.) What would you choose for them to touch, hold, make, see, hear, or use?

2   **Outside my world.** What have you learnt about in school that has been quite outside your experience? Other countries? History? The Romans? Stars and planets? Plays about people or places you have never encountered? Try to describe some of these things. What links with the things you have already experienced help you to understand them?

3   **The end.** Are you leaving school now? Look back over all those years when you *had* to go to school. Forget the grumbles. What are the happy memories? What has school meant to you? Describe some of the highlights — friends, games, fun, ideas, trips, jokes, exciting lessons, adventures.

24.7 Controversy

Would you be more careful if it was you that got pregnant?

Contraception is one of the facts of life.
Anyone, married or single, can get free advice on contraception from their doctor or family planning clinic.
You can find your local clinic under Family Planning in the telephone directory or Yellow Pages.

The Health Education Council
78 New Oxford Street, London WC1A 1AH.

**Head your work
24.7 Controversy
about experiences**

1   When a girl is pregnant, she and her husband should have to go to classes on how to bring up children.
2   All a small child needs is love.
3   We haven't had enough visits out of school to be able to understand the things we are meant to learn.
4   We *are* better qualified than pupils leaving school used to be.
5   It's been worth every penny of public money spent to keep us at school so long.

24.8 Read all about it

Many stories are written with animals or other creatures as the main characters. Some of these are books for small children, but some are definitely for adults. The author uses the imaginary creatures to make a pretend world that may, or may not, be something like our own. The story will certainly be fun to read; it may also give us a lot to think about.

J. R. R. Tolkien wrote a long story in three books called *The Lord of the Rings*. This is a book that thousands of young adults have been very keen on. He also wrote a shorter book called *The Hobbit*, which would be a good book to read first while you get to know his strange people — friendly and unfriendly — and his wonderful way of telling a story.

**Head your work
24.8 The world on
four feet**

Can you write a piece for adult reading (not for small children) in which you see our world and our manners through the eyes of animals — real or imaginary? If you follow the tradition of Tolkien or Orwell (or of Richard Adams in *Watership Down*), you will not need to explain how the animals can talk and run their own affairs — you just accept this and take the chance to comment on the ways of human beings.

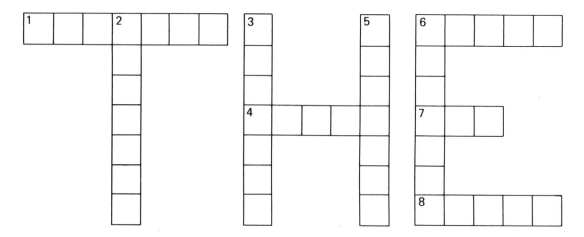

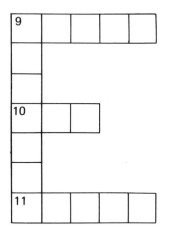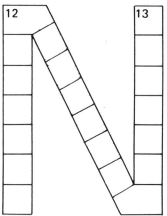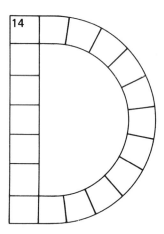

Clues across

* 1 The study of the past (7).
* 4 Quite plain, easy to understand (5).
* 6 A young person (5).
  7 To use your eyes (3).
* 8 Words that one can sing (5).
* 9 The capital city of Japan (5).
*10 To be able to do something (3).
*11 When ends of words sound the same (5).

Clues down

* 2 The author of 'The Hobbit' and 'The Lord of the Rings' (7).
* 3 To talk about something with another person (7).
* 5 Big American city where cars are made and trains bring food from the ranches (7).
* 6 Groups of pupils in a school (7).
* 9 Someone who is there to show you how to do it (7).

*12 The force that causes things to fall (7).
*12 (sloping) Complaints (8).
*13 Pupils who will not be coming to school any more after the end of term (7).
*14 To make-believe (7).
  14 (curved) Food that has been specially preserved (9, 4).

A note to
the teacher

This is a course book for non-academic pupils — both those who will be attempting some basic subjects, including English, in C.S.E., and those who will not be attempting a public examination. It aims to cover the essentials of good written and spoken English, and good reading, in a lively and relevant way.

The book tries to grasp the nettles firmly — it deals with basic phonics, reading speeds, simple and more extensive spelling problems, the use of a dictionary and punctuation rules. Every chapter contains several sections that have straight-forward reading; every chapter has a 'word-match' section to develop vocabulary, and a crossword which presents an opportunity to recapitulate on some of the harder words of the chapter.

Every chapter also has a section called 'controversy', with five provocative ideas, which can be used for debates, or class discussion, or talking points. Many of the other sections in each chapter can also be taken orally if the teacher feels the pupils will do themselves more justice this way — it is quite unnecessary for these pupils to do writing every day, but very important that they should become well skilled in clear discussion.

Although this aspect of the book is at a basic level, the ideas underlying the material are adult and demanding. There is no justification for assuming that a pupil who finds fluent reading or exact written work difficult should be debarred from discussing the aspects of adult life, employment, social reform or recreation that many of his peers are discussing. Nor is there any need to bow to the current vogue of concentrating on sordid, vulgar, or depressing social evils. An important feature of the book is the consistent policy of boosting these pupils' morale: not what they cannot do, but what they can; not 'down to their level', but 'up to their potential'.

Very specific divisions all through the book allow the teacher to pick out sections as required, and yet often leave a choice of written or oral treatment. Some tasks set are highly structured and tight, for pupils who require this degree of security, and yet every chapter also has some more open-ended work to allow the more adventurous ones some imaginative scope. Each chapter follows a regular pattern and yet care has been taken to make the approach varied and interesting.

But English teaching requires literature to feed on; and it is assumed that the class teacher will be bearing this in mind. The companion volume 'Need a Read?' brings together a wide selection of forms of literature arranged to run in parallel with the chapters of this book, although both 'English You Need', and 'Need a Read?', can stand perfectly well on their own also.

In 'Need a Read?' there are 24 short pieces that represent almost as many distinct forms of literature, and it is hoped that pupils will come to realize that some of these forms have a special appeal for them; and therefore want to look further at these types.

Altogether 'English You Need' contains 216 separate assignments, many with simple questions or discussion points attached, and also has suggestions for 72 short pieces of written work and a further 24 more imaginative pieces. There are 120 provocative points for debate, 24 crosswords and 13 riddles.

Thomas Nelson and Sons Ltd
Lincoln Way Windmill Road
Sunbury-on-Thames Middlesex
TW16 7HP

Thomas Nelson (Australia) Ltd
19–39 Jeffcott Street West
Melbourne Victoria 3003

Thomas Nelson and Sons (Canada) Ltd
81 Curlew Drive Don Mills Ontario

Thomas Nelson (Nigeria) Ltd
8 Ilupeju Bypass PMB 1303 Ikeja
Lagos

© Humphrey M. Dobinson 1978
First published 1978
Reprinted 1978
ISBN 0 17 433387 0

Filmset by Filmtype Services Ltd
Scarborough Yorkshire
Printed and bound in Hong Kong

Designed by Janet Sterling
Illustrations by: David Mostyn
                  Annie Bennet
                  Caroline Turner
                  Joanna Stubbs
                  Rowan Barnes-Murphy

Acknowledgements
Hundreds of people have helped in some way to make this book. Many have
helped without knowing it – pupils who have asked questions that show where
difficulties lie, or teachers who have discussed lessons with me. Others know they
have helped me, in particular my family. My thanks to them all.
For permission to reproduce copyright material grateful acknowledgements are
due to: Times Newspapers Limited for the article on Dr Sakharov which appeared
in *The Times* on 16th September 1976; *The Record* and Transport and General
Workers Union for 'Save our Milkmen'; Don Fair for 'Cricket pitches too small';
Frederick Warne (Publishers) Ltd for 'Looking after cats' from *The Observer's
Book of Cats* by Grace Pond; Richard Hughes Literary Estate and Chatto and
Windus Ltd for *A High Wind in Jamaica*; Laurence Pollinger Limited and the
Estate of the late Mrs Frieda Lawrence for *People*. The material on pp. 32–33 has
been adapted from *The Body and how it Works* by J. D. Ratcliff, published by
The Reader's Digest Association Limited, London, copyright © 1976.
Grateful acknowledgements for illustrations appearing on pages indicated are
due to: Barnaby's Picture Library (pp. 6, 16 top, 32, 39 top, 130, 133 top, 168);
Camera Press Ltd (pp. 12, 19, 39 bottom, 42, 43, 59, 144); Tony Othen (p. 16
bottom); Rex Features Ltd (p. 28); Mel Calman (p. 29); Humphrey M. Dobinson
(pp. 35, 71, 92 top, 94); Mary Evans Picture Library (p. 36); Exchange and Mart
(p. 40); The Post Office (p. 54 top and bottom); Keystone Press Agency Ltd
(pp. 60, 74, 81, 87, 88, 106); Heather Angel (p. 67 top and bottom); Sheelah
Latham (p. 72); The Mansell Collection (p. 73, 82, 95, 101, 102, 163, 164 top);
Syndication International (p. 75, 85, 86, 89, 121, 133 bottom); EMI Film
Distributors Ltd (p. 92 bottom); Oxford University Press (p. 98); from *Children's
Games in Street and Playground* by Iona and Peter Opie; Terry Williams (p. 99);
The RSPCA (p. 111); The National Gallery (p. 127); Chris Capstick (p. 128);
Curtis Brown Ltd and the Estate of E. H. Shepherd (pp. 20, 129, 131); Secker &
Warberg Ltd (p. 164 bottom); The Health Education Council (p. 172).
Every effort has been made to trace holders of copyright. It is hoped that any
omission will be pardoned.